JOHN JENKINS

Mayor
of Maine

CHUCK RADIS, D.O.

DownEastBooks

Camden, Maine

Down East Books

Published by Down East Books
An imprint of Globe Pequot
Trade division of The Rowman & Littlefield Publishing Group, Inc.
4501 Forbes Boulevard, Suite 200, Lanham, Maryland 20706
www.rowman.com

Distributed by NATIONAL BOOK NETWORK

ISBN 978-1-68475-085-6 (paperback)
ISBN 978-1-68475-086-3 (electronic)

♾️™ The paper used in this publication meets the minimum requirements of American National Standard for Information Sciences—Permanence of Paper for Printed Library Materials, ANSI/NISO Z39.48-1992.

Contents

Introduction

The inspiration for this book arose when close friends of John Jenkins formed a committee to develop a scholarship in his memory. Through the fund-raising efforts of this group, in partnership with Bates College, each year a Bates College minority student will receive financial aid toward their education. Members of this committee—Mel Donalson, Ann Parker, James Reese, Pam Wansker, Chuck James, Ira Waldman, Jill Bruce, and myself—met regularly by Zoom for more than a year and contributed photos and stories about John that have been included in this brief biography. As a member of this group, I volunteered to collect stories, edit them, and provide my own insights on what made John Jenkins an important figure in Maine politics and race relations.

It's fitting that this book is the product of those who knew John during different phases of his life. The stories and chapters follow the flow of his journey: Early years growing up in Newark, New Jersey; the Bates College Years; Martial Arts; Public Service; and his PepTalk experiences.

The stories about John kept coming in. Ren Halverson, Roger Blais, and Pam Wansker made Jenkins' years as a championship karate competitor come alive. Franco-American Ginger Levasseur generously spent time with me at her kitchen table and helped answer the question, "Why was John Jenkins so extraordinarily popular among Franco-American voters?" Many thanks also to Billy Johnson, who provided a memorable story linking Muhammad Ali and John Jenkins when the champ visited Lewiston for the 30th anniversary of the Ali-Liston World Championship bout. In the telling, Jenkins—who was then the mayor of Lewiston—demonstrated the grace, humor and pride in his adopted state that he was well known for.

Thanks also to Harold Williams, now in his 90s, who laughed and cried over his memories of John Jenkins on a wintry day in front of his wood stove in Auburn. Williams, a retired security guard at Bates

College, remembered how Jenkins' smile could always lower the temperature in any disagreement. It was Williams who said, "John Jenkins could say 'Go to hell' in such a manner that they would look forward to the trip."

Donna Card helped me remember Jenkins' over-the-top sense of humor with an outlandish tale of working with Jenkins at a store during the Christmas holidays when she was a high school student. The ability of Jenkins to hold an audience in the palm of his hand while dealing with unhappy customers suggests that he might have succeeded as a stand-up comedian.

Mujiba Wadud, John's sister who lives in Newark, New Jersey, provided an overview of her brother's childhood and what life was like in Newark during her brother's formative years. David Boone, a Bates College alumnus, recalled a meeting he had with Dean Lindholm and John Jenkins. Without David Boone's recommendation, it's unlikely Bates would have taken a chance on Jenkins. Francella Y. Trueblood, a cousin of Jenkins, now living in Salisbury, North Carolina, added a heart-felt perspective when she wrote, "His compassion had a way of rubbing off on those around him. He seemed to possess the 'it' (factor) that we see in people that is so hard to define."

My thanks also to Lewiston lawyer Elliot Epstein, who provided an overview of Lewiston politics and the economic decline of Lewiston/Auburn in the decades prior to Jenkins' terms as mayor. Phil Crowell, who has served the city of Auburn as a patrol officer, chief of police, and city manager, spent an hour with me during his busy day, recalling how Mayor Jenkins' leadership moved Auburn forward in times of great uncertainty. Phil Nadeau's book on the history of Lewiston, *The Unlikeliness of It All,* was an excellent source for understanding the Somali immigration to Lewiston in 2012.

Ann Parker, his fiancé and life partner, was invaluable in describing another side of John Jenkins few knew. Like many public figures, he was a private man who disclosed his innermost feelings to only a handful of friends.

Creating this book would not have been possible without Jim McCarthy, the former editor for the *Times Record* in Brunswick and a talented photographer. His advice and assistance added an artist's critical eye to the final layout and text. Thanks, also, to Russ Dillingham, a staff photographer for the *Lewiston Sun Journal*, who provided key photos documenting Jenkins' long career in Maine.

It was my pleasure to help organize and edit the stories that his friends have provided, and to add my own memories to this brief biography. John Jenkins' message for humanity holds important lessons today even as we strive toward a more perfect whole. The state of Maine is fortunate that he made Maine his home, and the story of his life is an important chapter in our state's history.

Chuck Radis, D.O.
Bates College, Class of 1975

Early Life in Newark, New Jersey

On March 27, 1968, 15-year-old Student Council President John Jenkins introduced the Reverend Martin Luther King Jr. at an assembly at South Side High School in Newark, New Jersey. King was on his way to march in solidarity with sanitation workers in Memphis, but made time in his busy schedule to meet with the students. One week later, Dr. King was assassinated as he stood on the balcony of the Lorraine Motel in Memphis, Tennessee, preparing to speak to Southern Christian Leadership Conference colleagues. At his funeral, Morehouse College President Benjamin Mays delivered the eulogy and mused that King "would probably say 'if death had to come, I am sure there was no greater cause to die for than fighting to get a just wage for garbage collectors.'"

The death of Dr. King had a profound effect on John Jenkins. Like many young men and women at South Side High School, his anger and frustration with racial injustice was at a boiling point. The previous summer, the city of Newark had erupted with the arrest of an African American cab driver by two white policemen when he drove his taxi around a police car and double-parked on 15th Avenue. During the brutal arrest, the driver suffered multiple injuries, but it was not until local civil rights leaders were allowed to see him in his holding cell, and saw the full extent of his injuries, that he was transferred to a nearby hospital for treatment.

The arrest and injuries of the cab driver fit an all-too-familiar pattern of police brutality. That evening, an angry crowd gathered across the street from the police precinct. Although local leaders urged the crowd to protest peacefully, a resident grabbed a bullhorn and spurred the crowd to action. Over the course of three days and nights, the city erupted in pent-up fury as fires and looting raged. The National Guard and State Police were called in. Before it was over, 26 people had died, and more than 700 had been injured.

On the eve of the riots, Newark had become one of the first Black-majority American cities, but remained under the control of white politicians. Property taxes were high and a steady stream of white Newark residents were fleeing to the suburbs where Blacks were often unable to obtain mortgages. The city was steadily losing population from its peak of 438,000 in 1950 to 381,000 in 1970. Infant and maternal mortality rates were the second highest in the nation. The school system was in disarray, placing it near the bottom of the state's ranking system. Racial profiling, redlining, and lack of equal opportunity in education, training, and jobs led the city's African American residents to feel powerless and disenfranchised.

It's not surprising that the Rev. Martin Luther King Jr.'s speech at South Side High School, with its emphasis on education and non-violent protest, was met with a mixed reception. Years later, Jenkins remembered, "Reverend King said if someone strikes you, turn the other cheek. And back then, I would say 'Yeah, you hit me and it's on.'" The words of activist Malcolm X, "Burn, baby, burn!" resonated with many in the Black community and became the mantra of those who argued the only way for Blacks to achieve equality in America was to set fire to the bonds of Black suppression. For a young Black man or woman, the choice between Malcolm X's vision and the Rev. Martin Luther King Jr.'s vision for the future was a difficult one.

This struggle for identity eventually played out on the local level. Following King's assassination, a number of high schools around the nation were renamed in honor of Martin Luther King Jr. In Newark, South Side High School was renamed Malcolm X Shabazz High for the fiery former Nation of Islam leader several years after Jenkins graduated.

At the age of 15, John Jenkins was at a crossroads. He could follow the teachings of Malcolm X; he could join a gang and descend into a life of hopelessness, violence, and anger; or he could find an alternative way forward. Dr. King's response to "Burn, baby, burn!" was to tell the audience at Jenkins's high school,

"Our slogan must not be Burn, baby, burn,
our slogan must be Learn, baby, learn,
so that we can earn, baby, earn!

Hearing the phrase made a lifelong impact on Jenkins. He later reflected, "Before he (King) spoke, I was more 'Burn, baby, burn!' but after, his message inspired me to have a dream worth working to achieve."

Who would have predicted that Jenkins' dream would bring him to Bates College in Lewiston, Maine, a state with the lowest percentage of minorities in the nation? It was at Bates College that John Jenkins came under the mentorship of Bates alumnus Benjamin Mays, who had delivered Rev. King's eulogy and was a prominent figure in the Civil Rights Movement. It was in Maine that John Jenkins set down roots, made lifelong friendships, successfully ran for office, and honed his unique brand of inspirational PepTalks that transformed the lives of so many he touched.

John Theodore Jenkins was born in Newark, New Jersey, on May 29, 1952. He was the middle child of Jane and John Jenkins Sr. and spent his formative years in a modest apartment building at 167

Johnson Avenue in a mixed neighborhood of Irish, Portuguese, and Italian immigrants. His grandparents lived upstairs, and several aunts and uncles were in nearby apartments. In the living room of the Jenkins apartment was a photo of an old man, a relative who had once been a slave. According to family lore, another uncle in the Deep South had agitated for the right to vote.

"They tarred and feathered him," Jenkins later recalled in an interview with Bill Nemitz of the *Portland Press Herald*. "They wanted to send a message."

His father, John Jenkins Sr., was a deacon in the nearby Baptist Church and prone to violence. In later years, Jenkins had little to say about his father. In an interview with Joshua Shea in the *Lewiston-Auburn* magazine in 2010, he summarized his relationship with the man by saying, "He was not consistently present in my life." His older sister, Mujiba, recalled a darker side to their parents' relationship. On one occasion, their mother was beaten so severely by their father that she was taken to the hospital. It was after this, that they divorced. Jenkins was 7 years old.

Mujiba believed that witnessing the beatings had a profound effect on Teddy (John's family nickname). "He didn't want to end up like his dad."

His mother, Jane, also a Baptist, strove to instill in all of the Jenkins children a strict moral code. She recognized the critical importance of keeping her children engaged and off the streets, particularly during the long, hot summers when school was not in session. As Jenkins later recalled, "I was raised by a loving and totally committed single mother of faith . . . (and) her faith literally was my life's salvation until I learned how to believe on my own." His mother enrolled him in his first karate class at age 10. He also joined the Boy Scouts. "My mother didn't know anything about those two programs. The only thing she heard was the magic word—discipline."

In Newark, violence and tragedy were never far away. Reflecting on his childhood, Jenkins said, "One day I remember hanging out on a street corner with one of my friends. I had some place to go to, a scouting meeting or something, and I left him. A minute after I left, my friend got caught in the middle of some dispute he wasn't a part of and was killed. I just knew if it wasn't for those organized activities it could have been me. In the neighborhood, money got you respect, because it got you the newest and the best stuff. You saw the gangsters with the cars and the jewelry. If not for my mother and a few honorable men who stepped up to the plate and unknowingly became my male role models, it would have been easy to fall into that life."

The young Jenkins was curious, outrageously funny, athletic, and accident-prone. At 11, he injured himself falling out of bed. Another time, he wandered into a clump of bushes, and was stung by a swarm of bees so severely he was admitted to the hospital for treatment. His sister Mujiba recalled, "He was like a cat with nine lives."

There is no simple explanation for why one young man hangs out on the corner while another embraces the challenges and high expectations of scouting or the martial arts. Not every scouting troop or martial arts class has the right mix of leadership, concern, and high expectations to keep a young man engaged. Sometimes, life moves forward with the simple act of showing up. John showed up. In a *Lewiston Sun Journal* interview in 2015, Jenkins said that scouting introduced him to the outdoors. Karate fine-tuned his body and mind. Both gave him something to focus on and excel at other than roaming the streets of Newark.

Recalling one of his earliest experiences with karate, Jenkins watched as a group of students began doing kata forms. "Suddenly, I saw this group of people all moving in unison. No one was showing each other how to make that next step. It was as if they had one mind. I had never seen, en masse, a group of people look [in] the same direction and make the next move. I was like, how did they do that? My mouth stopped running, and my eyes and ears opened." Jenkins pored over karate magazines and began to dream. In his high school yearbook, he wrote, "Some day, I want to be a world champion." It was not a casual comment. The high expectations of his mentors and his inner drive spurred his progress, step by step, toward greater mastery of the martial arts.

He rejected the temptation and camaraderie of a tight-knit gang as a substitute for family. His mother and siblings and extended family, along with his success and acceptance in the world of scouting and the martial arts, provided him with the emotional support he sorely needed as a young man. "I realized that maybe these activities were keeping me alive. There was always more to learn. I was able to physically do things because of the training. I saw the benefits immediately. I was thinking more clearly. I had a better sense of how to gauge difficult situations and difficult people. I no longer felt the need to run away."

His newfound prowess was rarely expressed in fighting outside the confines of the dojo. As his confidence grew on the streets of Newark, Jenkins began to explore alternatives to violence by de-escalating everyday confrontations with self-deprecating humor and deflection.

"Timing, patience, and focus—all those things in your training in the martial arts gets applied to daily social interactions," he later recalled. "It's the living arts."

Throughout his adolescence, his mother worked multiple jobs to sustain the family. One summer, his mother helped him land a job at a factory in Bellville, New Jersey, where grocery store smocks were repaired and cleaned. "My mother was in charge of a giant steam presser machine and maybe in the winter it wasn't bad, but in the summer it was unbearable. On Day 1, I wimped out and I quit. I couldn't take it. It's just one of the jobs she had at the time."

"Once, in my early teen years, I remember complaining to my mom how I desperately needed her to purchase me a fashionable knit shirt. She said that she would love to buy me that shirt, but times were tough, and we could barely afford the next rent payment. I said, 'I'm sick and tired of being poor.' She sighed and shook her head slowly before replying. 'Son, it is true our current finances are limited. Yes, we do live in some challenging conditions. But you must come to know that we are not poor. Poor is an attitude. If you think you are that, then you will always be that.'"

And then her final magic statement: "Learn to see beyond your circumstances."

His mother, Jane, understood that Scouts and the martial arts would take her young son only so far unless he also excelled in his studies. Although South Side High School at one time had an excellent academic reputation—graduating future New York City Mayor Ed Koch, by the time Jenkins attended, academic expectations had declined. Even so, John Jenkins' goal from an early age was to become a doctor.

In 1968, months after Rev. King was assassinated, Mrs. Jenkins, with the help of church connections, arranged for her 16-year-old son to attend Princeton University's Cooperative Summer School program, designed to expose students from disadvantaged backgrounds to post-secondary education. The following summer, he was accepted into an Upward Bound Trio Program in Lowell, Massachusetts. The experiences shaped and molded his natural ability to connect with people from a wide variety of backgrounds and honed the leadership qualities he had already shown glimpses of as student council president.

The two programs expanded his world even as the quality of his South Side High School public education went into freefall. In 1970, Jenkins' senior year, South Side was closed for three weeks due to teach-ers' strikes. This gap barely scratched the surface of what was actually happening in the classroom. Frequent teacher absences and slow-downs, picket lines and violence, both inside and outside of South Side, were a part of Jenkins' everyday school experience. At a time when college pre-paratory classes such as algebra, pre-calculus, and chemistry should have been laying the foundation for college success, education in Newark came to a grinding halt. The teachers' union grievances were legitimate; they struck for better pay and a voice in the curriculum. However, the timing of the strikes could not have come at a worse time for Jenkins.

As a result of the strikes, almost 200 teachers were arrested and jailed. In what may have been John Jenkins' first act of civil disobedi-ence, he organized a sit-in at the school superintendent's office in New-ark to draw attention to the real victims in the struggle between the teachers' union and the city of Newark: the students. The local police were called to remove the demonstrators, who did not voluntarily leave the office. The police then bound the demonstrators' wrists and dragged them from the building by their ankles—down the steps of the four-story building.

Through his success at the summer programs at Princeton and the Upward Bound Program in Lowell, Massachusetts, a growing number of colleges were aware of John Jenkins. He had demonstrated leader-ship at South Side High School through his presidency of the student council. Karate had transformed his 5-foot-9-inch frame into a mus-cular, 200-pound Black Hercules. He was a running back on a football team that had sent several players on to the NFL. According to his close friend, Ren Halverson, who later trained and competed with John in karate, Jenkins had several offers to play football at Division 1 schools. Halverson remarked, "His leg drive from those thighs of his reminded me of a thoroughbred breaking out of the starting gate. The shoulder pads I thought I saw the first day in Portland (Maine) warming up were his shoulders. Massive chest, no fat—you get the picture."

Bates College Black alumni brothers David and Nate Boone became aware of Jenkins, perhaps through Roscoe Lee, another South Side High School graduate who was enrolled at Bates. The Boone brothers often recruited students for Bates and demonstrated a sincere interest in Jenkins, often attending his athletic events. They arranged a meeting with Milt Lindholm, the dean of admissions at Bates, in New York City. Between his dream of becoming a doctor and his goal of becoming a world champion in karate, Jenkins must have made quite an impression.

David Boone remembers the interview: "He was very confident about his abilities. He had the gift of gab and was jovial and outgoing. When we were done, it felt like you'd known him all your life. There were no airs." At the conclusion of the interview, Dean Lindholm put together a financial package that would make admission to Bates College a reality. What was left unsaid was the question of whether Jenkins could succeed at college level academics. Between the trauma of the Newark riots and the gaps in Jenkins' education at South Side High School, there must have been concern that he lacked the foundation for a Bates College education.

In typical understatement, Jenkins later recalled, "That was a gamble on their part." David Boone remembers having no such reservations. "If Bates admitted him, I was confident he'd get through."

2

Academic Challenges—
The Bates College Years

Before deciding to attend Bates, Jenkins, who did not have a driver's license, took a bus to Maine for a visit to the college in Lewiston. A student guide gave the young Jenkins a tour among the majestic elms lining the campus walkways. They might have stopped at the "pond," a shallow body of water nestled between two dormitories,

where generations of (inebriated) Bates students have traditionally cut a hole in the ice and plunged into the freezing water in celebration of winter. At the time, Jenkins, who did not know how to swim, was likely not impressed by this unusual tradition. If he had met another Black student that day, he would have seen a significant percentage of the total Black enrollment at Bates. The tour ended at the school cafeteria, where Jenkins loaded up his tray with multiple entrees and desserts. When his tray was empty, the guide assured him that he could go up for seconds, or even thirds. Soon after that visit, John Jenkins committed to attend Bates College.

At first glance, Bates College, a small liberal arts institution in the gritty mill town of Lewiston, Maine, would seem to be an unlikely destination for an inner-city African American student. With an enrollment of less than 1,500 students, the college was smaller than Newark's South Side High School, and as Maine's second largest city at 41,000, Lewiston would qualify in New Jersey as a medium-sized town.

But with equality built into its founding DNA, Bates offered the young Jenkins a supportive environment to learn and grow. The college was established in 1855 as a Free Baptist institution, and from its

John Jenkins walks with his mentor, Benjamin E. Mays, and former Bates College President T. Hedley Reynolds at the college campus. *(Courtesy Bates College)*

inception strove toward the goal of racial and gender equality. Bates was the first coeducational college in New England and prided itself on admitting students without regard to race, religion, national origin, or gender. During the Civil War, the college sheltered runaway Black slaves and later graduated its first African American, Henry Wilkens Chandler in 1873—only three years after Harvard College became the first college in the nation to break the color barrier by awarding a degree to another Black man, Richard T. Greener (who later became a philosophy professor, law school dean and foreign diplomat).

By the time Jenkins arrived at Bates in the fall of 1970, Lewiston was in deep economic decline. Textile jobs had moved overseas to lower-cost factories in China and Japan. The mills, which once had hummed with the activity of French-Canadian immigrant workers, were empty. Unemployment was high and a long line of businesses on Lewiston's Lisbon Street were bankrupt and shuttered.

The country was mired in the Vietnam War, and protests were widespread. The assassinations of President John F. Kennedy in 1963, Malcolm X in 1965, Dr. Martin Luther King in 1968, and Robert F. Kennedy in 1968, had deepened racial wounds in an already divided nation. Despite the recent passage of the Civil Rights Act by Congress in 1964, only four years before John Jenkins matriculated at Bates College, George Wallace had run for the presidency of the United States as an avowed white supremacist, winning the popular vote in four states.

The twin cities of Lewiston-Auburn had their own history of ethnic and racial discrimination. "If anyone walks down Lisbon Street in Lewiston, he will certainly think that he is in . . . an alien land, where foreigners speaking a strange language are everywhere," an observer claimed. "There are 'few real Americans' left in the city," another man griped. The "aliens" the writers had vilified in the "Maine Klansman" were immigrants from Quebec, speaking French and practicing what some natives viewed as a dangerous (Catholic) religion. The year was 1924.

The Ku Klux Klan and their message of white Protestant superiority resonated with some residents in Lewiston and in Maine at large. French Canadians were viewed as a threat, in part due to their large numbers and the perception they were taking jobs from "real" Americans. There were few Blacks in Maine, but they also experienced day-to-day discrimination. In 1970, there were only 2,816 Blacks out of a state population of 993,663, a fraction of 1 percent. It was not until John Jenkins' freshman year at Bates College that Gerald Talbot became the first Black to be elected to the Maine State Legislature. Several years before he assumed office, Talbot brought a successful lawsuit against the landlord of an apartment who refused to rent to him, saying he would "burn the apartment before renting it to a nigger."

At the time of Talbot's entry into politics, Black politicians were winning elections in many districts across the United States, but primarily in Black-majority towns and cities. Gerald Talbot's ability to form successful coalitions with like-minded white Maine Democrats and Independents was the key to his election success. Talbot's prominence enabled him to bring attention to deeply entrenched bias in state government, not only against Blacks but also against French-Canadians and Native Americans. It would not be the last time that a Black politician in Maine would gain the critical support of the French-Canadian community.

At Bates, even if overt racism was rare, Black students on campus knew they were not welcome by some white students. David Boone, the man most responsible for shepherding Jenkins to Bates, remembers "the frowners" during his college years in the early 1960s. "There were fellow students who didn't want to have us on campus. We felt it. We knew who they were."

When John Jenkins arrived by bus on the Bates College campus in 1970, the culture shock was overwhelming. In a *Lewiston-Auburn* magazine interview 40 years later, he remembered thinking, "Where are all the Black and Spanish people . . . and how can I purchase the cultural products I'm used to?" But the transition also triggered an unexpected reaction: "Why is it all so quiet? In Newark, you're always hearing vehicles, sirens, people fighting, dogs barking. It's a constant barrage. I remember running upstairs in my dorm to a couple of guys who lived above me. They were pretty studious, and I asked, 'Do you guys hear that?' They said they didn't hear anything, and I said, 'That's the problem! I don't hear anything either. It's too silent!'"

Fortunately, there was also significant support for freshman John Jenkins. He developed a friendship with a Bates College Black alumnus, Benjamin Elijah Mays, class of 1920. As president of Morehouse

College in Atlanta, Mays mentored the Rev. Martin Luther King Jr., who called Mays "my spiritual mentor and my intellectual father." Former U.S. Ambassador to the United Nations Andrew Young said of Mays' pivotal relationship with Martin Luther King Jr., "There would have been no King if not for Benjamin Mays."

Although Mays grew up in the segregated south, he experienced his share of humiliation in the north as well. On one occasion, he was invited to speak at the United Baptist Church on Main Street in Lewiston in front of a crowd estimated at 750. Organizers of the event (wary of the racial climate of Lewiston) asked the manager of the nearby DeWitt Hotel whether there would be a problem with Mays' inclusion at a celebratory dinner that night in the main dining room. According to a *Lewiston Sun* article published at the time, the manager, Allen Browne, recommended that it would be a mistake to allow Mays to eat in the public dining room. He recalled that a few years earlier, some Bates professors and African American guests had eaten in the main dining hall at the hotel, causing several Lewiston and Auburn women to leave the room in a huff, refusing to pay for the meals they had ordered.

The next day, the *Sun Journal* criticized the hotel for turning Mays away: "We have faith in Lewiston people and know they generally disapprove of acts which smack of race prejudice." The newspaper urged those involved "to clear the city's name of any possible charge of inhospitality to such a distinguished gentleman as Dr. Mays."

Two years after the incident at the DeWitt Hotel, Mays was asked to be a Bates College trustee and was awarded an honorary doctor of divinity degree. In his autobiography, *Born to Rebel*, Mays highlighted the critical importance of his Bates College education: "Bates College did not 'emancipate' me; it did the far greater service of making it possible for me to emancipate myself, to accept with dignity my own worth as a free man. Small wonder that I love Bates College!"

When John Jenkins matriculated at Bates, Benjamin Mays was a vibrant 76 years old, and head of the Atlanta Board of Education where he presided over the difficult task of desegregating the city's school system. Mays traveled to Lewiston regularly and felt a deep responsibility to pass on his philosophy of racial justice to incoming Black men and women at Bates College.

His support and influence were often subtle, but Mays could also be painfully direct. From long experience, Mays knew that protest alone was insufficient to change the status quo. He challenged African American students at Bates to develop organizational strategies, including detailed charts, on how to achieve a particular goal. For example, an important goal of the newly formed Afro-American Society at Bates was to attract more Black students and professors to Bates, but to do so required an environment that celebrated Black culture. Protest alone was unlikely to produce lasting change. To make lasting progress required collaboration with the Bates College student body, faculty, and administration.

Years later, thinking back on his friendship with Mays, Jenkins said, "I thought people befriended you because they could get something from you. I had nothing to give Dr. Mays, yet he would sit with me for hours to talk about life. Mays focused on your personhood. I've tried to live by that, taking time for any student anytime there's a question."

One of John Jenkins' most treasured possessions was an autographed copy of Mays' book, *Born to Rebel.* Jenkins later wrote, "The 'riches' of relationships occur when we are open, curious, and willing to listen. There seems to be an energy or force opening doors and guiding me forward when no 'way' seemed possible. I need to continue working on remaining faithful, focused, and fit for the challenges ahead."

Major adjustments were in store for freshman John Jenkins in the fall of 1970. Classmate Pam Wansker remembers, "When John arrived at Bates, plain and simple, he didn't like white people." Another friend, Ren Halverson, had a slightly different take on John's racial views. "He said something along the lines of 'It's not that I dislike white folks, I really didn't know many very well that weren't criminals in my neighborhood.'" In another conversation several years later, as he saw Jenkins adapt to Maine's overwhelmingly white culture, Halverson remembers Jenkins saying, "There are racial jerks everywhere in the world but we all need to see the human race for what it is. There are two types of people, those who sit around complaining that they didn't get the breaks, and those who make the breaks through study, work, applying themselves, and treating others as the Golden Rule says. Anything else fails to justify

Lord,
The People Have Driven Me On

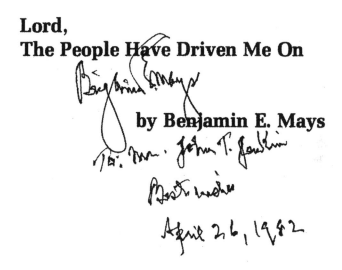

Benjamin E. Mays

by Benjamin E. Mays

To: Mr. John T. Jenkins

Best wishes

April 26, 1982

VANTAGE PRESS
New York / Washington / Atlanta
Los Angeles / Chicago

Benjamin E. Mays, a Class of 1920 alumnus of Bates College who the Rev. Martin Luther King Jr. once described as "my spiritual mentor and my intellectual father," befriended Jenkins during his occasional visits to the Lewiston campus as a college trustee.

not getting off your butt and realizing God gives everyone the same opportunity, albeit not the same set of circumstances."

The comments reflected the message from the Rev. Martin Luther King Jr's speech to the South Side High School assembly in Newark in 1968. Instead of 'Burn, baby, burn!" Jenkins had come to believe that the key to racial equality was "Learn, baby, learn."

Somewhat surprisingly, in his first year on campus, Jenkins was not universally accepted by his Black classmates, some of whom were the sons and daughters of lawyers and physicians and had attended private schools. At pre-season football practice, Black teammate Mel Donalson, who would become one of Jenkins' closest friends, recalled his initial impression of the young Jenkins: "I didn't like him at first. He was annoying. He used to come over to my dorm room in his underwear, turn up the music and dance and sing while I tried to study. Who is this guy? When he stopped coming in, I missed him."

As a Division III liberal arts college, Bates did not award athletic scholarships, but instead provided financial aid based on need. Maintaining a football team, even if it was not championship caliber, was critical to the college's philosophy of encouraging students to succeed both on the playing field and in the classroom.

His first fall at Bates, Jenkins adjusted to a new role on the football team: bench warmer. He was often injured and did not win the starting offensive back position. Teammate Bob Littlefield recalled on a Bates College podcast in October 2020: "We shared a position and John didn't get a boat-load of playing time. But he made an indelible impression right away. He was boisterous, positive and funny. His laugh was infectious—and he laughed a lot. In general, it's the stars of the team who lead the team; John, even though he didn't have much playing time, was definitely one of our leaders. Some of us started calling him the Mayor of Bates College."

Although he made light of his lack of playing time, in private he wondered if race played a role, as he noticed that he and another Black player, Roscoe Lee, were never on the playing field at the same time. Teammate Ira Waldman had another take on why John Jenkins saw limited minutes on the field: "He fumbled the ball frequently. You don't play much if you can't hold onto the ball."

John Jenkins' goal was to become a physician and to return to Newark to practice, and he began the fall semester of 1970 at Bates with a heavy load of math and science pre-medical classes. As his freshman year unfolded, however, it was clear that he was in over his head. Unlike many Bates freshmen who had excelled at advanced math and science classes in high school, Jenkins soon discovered that South Side High School had not prepared him for the rigors of a pre-medical education.

He struggled with and eventually failed organic chemistry, a critical course for pre-medical students. Bates' high academic expectations for its students left little room for remedial classes. Between his disappointment on the gridiron and the painful reality of failing organic chemistry, Jenkins might well have wondered: Do I belong here? Are these my people?

By Thanksgiving break of freshman year, it was clear that Jenkins was at a crossroads. His dream of becoming a physician was at risk. Failing organic chemistry wasn't his only disappointment; calculus was also proving to be impenetrable. The two classes must have been like learning a foreign language with the expectation he would be fluent in a matter of months. He changed majors from biology to psychology but worried that unless he kept his overall grade average above 2.0 (the equivalent of a C average), he could be expelled from school.

Classmate Karen Harris-Gipps agreed to pick up Jenkins in Newark on her way back to Bates after spending the holidays with her family in New Jersey. She knew that it had been a difficult semester for Jenkins but didn't know how close he was to flunking out. She drove into Newark and passed block after block of burned-out buildings. More than three years after the riots, almost nothing had been torn down or rebuilt. Her directions to Jenkins' apartment were vague. She worried she would not find him in the maze of city streets. On a deserted corner was a shiny telephone booth, untouched, in the midst of the inner-city devastation. Just beyond the phone booth, suitcase in hand, John Jenkins waited to be picked up.

That winter, classwork continued to be a major challenge but Jenkins slowly adjusted to Bates, or, perhaps, the Bates community might have adjusted to him. He joined the fledgling Afro-American Society, which had been created the year before by several Black students:

Marilyn Nixon, Mel Donalson, Roscoe Lee, and Walt Toombs. John participated in the club and helped to establish the group and its programs on firm footing.

Additionally, he was recruited by coach Walter Slovenski to run indoor track, but similar to his experience in football, he was not the star of the team. John Emerson, an outstanding miler at Bates, remembers Jenkins as "larger than life, curious about his teammates, and relentlessly upbeat. He was a man who loved people and people loved him." Emerson, who married at 19, was the father of two children by the time he graduated. Similar to Jenkins, academics did not come easily to Emerson. As the Bates mile record holder, the pressure of competition also weighed heavily on him. Observing the antics of John Jenkins at track practice, as he needled the weight men and joked with the distance runners, helped Emerson adjust his focus and to better enjoy the camaraderie of the track team.

In track, as in other sports, groups form: shot putters and hammer throwers hang with other weight men; sprinters with sprinters and milers with milers. Jenkins was everywhere at practices and at meets. As a self-appointed coach, he provided advice, some of it hilarious, to All-American hammer thrower Bob Cedrone, giving pointers on balance and explosiveness based on his long experience in karate—even though before enrolling at Bates, the only hammer John Jenkins had held was used to pound nails into a piece of wood.

On the outside, John Jenkins seemed well-adjusted to campus life. He was making friends and becoming well-known at Bates for his outrageous sense of humor and openness to new experiences. But like so many college freshmen, he was still searching for community, a place where he could let down his guard and be the person he was striving to be. He missed the discipline, camaraderie, and sense of purpose that karate had provided him as a ten-year-old in Newark. His search led him to the Golden Fist on Pine Street, about a mile from campus. There, he was introduced to the owner, Richard Gates, a balding, highly skilled blackbelt with an eye for fresh talent, who immediately asked Jenkins to change into his gi and participate in the traditional kata with the other students. Roger Blais, a fellow student who would later earn a black belt of his own, remembers, "That first day that John changed into his blue-silk gi, he moved with such grace and power, he made an immediate impact."

Jenkins' connection with the Golden Fist filled a critical gap in his life. In the classroom, despite his intense efforts, he was falling behind. In football and track, despite his powerful build, he often fell short of his high expectations. Karate was somehow different. The internal journey and philosophy made perfect sense to him. And he was shockingly good at it.

At the time, it was unusual for Bates students to meet and mix with Lewiston residents. An unspoken "town versus gown" mentality kept the two groups largely apart. Bates students rarely volunteered or worked in the surrounding community and, compared to today's relationship between Bates students and Lewiston-Auburn, the college did not expect students to perform community service. Bates students sometimes maligned their Lewiston peers as less intelligent, less educated, and prone to violence. In turn, "townies" viewed Bates students as elitist and effete. If they mingled at all, it was in the bars down the hill from the Bates campus, sometimes with disastrous results.

"It was really difficult for most Bates students to integrate in the community because most of the people spoke French and lived a hard life," remembers Peter Heyel, who graduated from Bates shortly before Jenkins began his studies. "Looking back, when I think about why we wouldn't integrate, it was us who didn't belong."

Jenkins initially connected with Lewiston's Franco-Americans at the Bates Commons, where he worked part-time in the kitchen, restocking the shelves or working as a dishwasher. Many of the full-time employees in the cafeteria were former Franco-American mill workers who were grateful for the work, even if it didn't require the exacting skills they'd mastered in the now-shuttered local textile mills. Jenkins worked in a back room at the cafeteria where a conveyor belt delivered trays filled with glasses and dirty dishes. He would give the dishes an initial rinse before placing them in an industrial-sized dishwasher. It was a wet, dirty job.

It was not unusual to hear John's cackling laughter and distinctive voice mixing and rising above the lilting French-Canadian accents. One classmate remembered: "They laughed along with John and absolutely loved working alongside him. Singing while working was common-place. John made people feel so comfortable that even the older women flirted with him, hoping to gain his friendship. And more than once I would catch a glance from a worker with a twinkle in her eye and a coy grin as she watched John. He seemed to distract them from the tedium of the work. He even managed to get the clicker lady—a stern-looking woman with a clicker who stood at the cafeteria entrance checking Bates IDs—to break out in a grin."

Perhaps it was his friendship with his Franco-American co-workers at Bates which encouraged John Jenkins to venture outside the Bates campus into downtown Lewiston. Perhaps the vibrant Franco-American culture in downtown Lewiston reminded him of his own community in Newark, New Jersey (At the time, Franco-Americans comprised roughly 70 percent of the population of the Lewiston/Auburn twin cities, many of them living in what was known as "Little Canada" on the Lewiston side of the Androscoggin River).

Compared to the Bates campus, Little Canada was the opposite of quiet. The odor along the canals lining the Androscoggin River was pungent, music blared from the run-down tenements, dogs barked, sirens blew. Instead of the music of the Temptations or Aretha Franklin or Stevie Wonder, the rhythms of guitars and fiddles played by Franco-Americans drifted out of nearby bars. It was a connection that would play out again and again in John Jenkins' life.

But even after switching from pre-medical science classes to psy-chology, and despite the support of his growing circle of friends in Lewiston and in the Bates community, Jenkins continued to struggle academically. By the end of the fall semester of sophomore year, his cumulative grade point average had fallen below a C average, and he was temporarily expelled from Bates. For some students, the embar-rassment of flunking out would have ended their college studies. John Jenkins was undeterred.

He decided to remain in Lewiston in hopes of resuming his studies after Christmas vacation. Jobs in his hometown of Newark were scarce, and he may have felt that if he returned home, he might never come back. With the loss of his part-time student job at the Bates cafeteria, he became both a pupil and teacher at the Golden Fist. His connection to the Golden Fist could not have come at a more critical time; if his grades at Bates had been a disappointment, his progress in karate was nothing short of remarkable. Fueled by an iron will to continue his studies at Bates, he poured himself into the martial arts.

That winter, despite the money he earned as an instructor at the Golden Fist, John Jenkins could not afford the rent on an apartment in Lewiston. He was homeless, and couch-surfed around the Bates College campus. Classmate Pam Wansker remembers hearing that on some wintry nights he slept outside on a bench on the Bates quad, covering himself with newspapers to stay warm. The experience humbled him, but he somehow retained his sense of humor.

3

Resilience

Donna Card, a high school senior in Lewiston at the time, remembers working with John Jenkins on the Saturday before Christmas in 1972 at Service Merchandise. For its time, Service Merchandise was very high-tech: when customers decided on an item, they pulled off the tag and handed it to a cashier, who placed the ticket inside a hydraulic tube. In moments, the ticket arrived at the warehouse in the back; a worker pulled the item from the shelf and sent it back to the front area on a conveyor belt to be cashed out.

But not that day. Something had gone wrong in the warehouse. The conveyor belt was still. Card stood at her cash register looking out at a sea of agitated customers waiting for their merchandise to arrive. People were getting ugly. Kids were getting fidgety. One little boy started to cry; then he *really* started to wail. Co-worker John Jenkins whispered to Card that they were lucky to be behind the counter instead of out in that angry mob.

Suddenly, Jenkins made a show of sending another order up the tube, but pretended his arm was stuck in the tube. He struggled a little, "trying" to pull his arm out, and apologized to everyone, but seeing he now had the boy's attention (and everyone else's) he really got into being stuck. He thrashed and pulled, but his arm remained "stuck" in the tube. Well, the "audience" was on to him now, and some began to snicker. That's all the encouragement he needed. Jenkins wailed and yelled for help. He twisted and flailed and wailed some more, begging co-worker Donna Card for help, grabbing her to keep him from being sucked up the tube. "Please help me, why are you just standing there laughing? This isn't funny!" Uncontrolled laughter spread up and down the line. People were laughing so hard they held onto each other to keep from falling.

Finally, the manager was told by the warehouse that the conveyor belt problem had been fixed and whispered to John, "You can stop. *John. you can stop now!"* Jenkins made a big show of pulling his arm out (as if that bicep could fit in the tube, right?) and profusely thanked the warehouse guy who had "fixed" the problem and had "saved" him, shaking his hand, hugging him and just being ridiculously over-the-top. He then took a bow and graciously went on to cash out customers, apologizing for the delay and thanking them for shopping at Service Merchandise.

When he was readmitted to Bates in early 1973, John Jenkins penned an article for the Bates student newspaper about his struggle at

the college, both in the classroom and on the athletic fields. Describing his experiences on the gridiron, he wrote, "I earned the unofficial title of 'The Bobcat Cowboy'—that is, I rode the pine. I rode so much that I used to carry my own special pair of tweezers to the game, so I could pull out splinters during the team's time-outs. Things got to the point that I stopped expecting to play and would suit up just to be pretty for the fans."

Regarding track, he wrote, "You get a funny feeling when you're running as fast as you can, and some wise girl on the side yells out so everyone can hear, 'Hey, hey, hey! Look at the fat boy in the back!' You get a funny feeling when you come out of the starting block and you look up, and you see all your competition twenty yards ahead of you in the 60-yard dash."

Hamming it up at the Lobster Festival in Rockland, John Jenkins performs a stunt that he had used years earlier to defuse angry customers at the Service Merchandise store, where he worked during the pre-Christmas shopping season in 1972. The self-deprecating humor Jenkins learned during his younger years in Newark, New Jersey, is a skill he put to good use his entire life.

Nearing the end of the essay, he shared his academic struggles with the student body:

You get a funny feeling when you just know you did well on a test until you get it back.

You get a funny feeling when you know Mr. Lindholm (Bates Director of Admissions) has made another mistake.

You get a funny feeling when you try for yourself and for those who have faith in you, and you don't make it.

You get a funny feeling when you really think you're sure about something, and you find out that you're not sure about anything.

You get a funny feeling when you develop a closeness with people who have become dear to you, and suddenly that attachment is severed.

You get a funny feeling when you don't even know why you're feeling funny.

Referring to his temporary expulsion from Bates the previous semester, his resilience was on display in his closing remarks:

Anyway, I am grateful for the opportunity to have experienced this pause in my life, and maybe everyone to some extent needs a pause of some sort in their lives. I tried it and I like it, but now business goes on as usual.

Humbly yours, John Jenkins.

That winter, a more determined John Jenkins settled into his studies. Although he had struggled with higher math and chemistry, psychology had become a comfortable fit. His off-the-charts social IQ found the study of human behavior captivating, and he poured himself into the new major. The dream of attending medical school was put on hold but not extinguished. Taking the long view, he knew that not all physicians traveled a straight line from college to medical school. Some took a meandering course, majoring in art or the social sciences in college before picking up the required basic science classes and sitting for the all-important medical college entrance exam test (MCAT).

In the meantime, Jenkins immersed himself in the Bates community. He dated Pam Wansker, a white classmate at Bates, who taught him how to drive her ancient Volkswagen "bug." Growing up poor in Newark, driver's education was unaffordable, and until coming to Bates, the lack of a driver's license had never been a liability. Jenkins was anxious to learn, and it was not long before he was able to obtain a driver's license.

He progressed rapidly in his classes and in his dual role as an instructor at the Golden Fist. Pam Wansker attended classes at the

John Jenkins and Pam Wansker, a classmate at Bates College who taught him how to drive her Volkswagen "bug" so that he could get his first driver's license.

Golden Fist. So did Mel Donalson, a Black football teammate, who eventually earned a black belt. Fellow Bates students Al Gardner and Mark Delaney, and Lewiston native Roger Blais, often competed with Wansker and Jenkins in out-of-state tournaments as far away as New York City and Cleveland. Now that John had a driver's license, he shared in the long drives home, crammed into the undersized VW bug. They listened to Richard Pryor or George Carlin tapes on the cassette player, memorizing the punch lines and howling with laughter. At dawn after an all-night drive, Pam Wansker remembers the sun coming up on the Maine Turnpike, the windshield rimmed with ice. "John loved to laugh, and laughing with him was infectious."

After one successful New York City tournament, before the long drive home, Sensei Masakazu Takahashi invited the group out for dinner at a Chinese restaurant. Takahashi ordered an enormous whole fish, and when it arrived, pointed to Jenkins, who had won the tournament. "Eat eye," he told Jenkins. "Make you strong!" An uncomfortable silence hovered over the table. Finally, Jenkins grabbed his fork and poking the eye out of the fish, prepared to down the eye. "No, No, No!" Sensei Takahashi blurted out, catching the fork with his free hand. "Joke! Big joke!"

Jenkins' interest in new experiences was legendary. With considerable difficulty, he learned how to swim. Ren Halverson remembers: "Guys with muscle mass like a Tyrannosaurus Rex don't float well. In his case, he sank like a cinder block." His instructors tried every technique they could think of to make him more buoyant; none of them worked. In Maine, John Jenkins had plenty of company. Many lobstermen, even after a lifetime on the water, never learned to swim.

Despite his swimming limitations, one summer he was hired as a lifeguard by the city of Auburn. As one classmate recalled, "He was excellent with beach duty; he would entertain the kids and play games with them, but he always had the life buoy float to use if someone struggled in the water . . . and he made sure another guard was nearby in case the need for a deep-water rescue arose."

Even with his switch to psychology, classes at Bates continued to be a challenge for Jenkins. Unlike some schools such as Harvard, where professors reportedly almost never assigned a grade lower than a B-plus, grade inflation at Bates was non-existent. In the same issue of the 1973 *Bates Student* in which John Jenkins wrote about his athletic and academic struggles at Bates, reporter Karen Olson noted, "One-fourth of the freshman class received academic warning after their first semester at Bates this year—approximately 90 out of 361. Figures are not yet completed for the other three classes; however, 12 students have been dismissed and a larger number placed on academic probation."

Critical thinking was an important component of a Bates College liberal arts education and mastering the skills of analysis and interpretation was an acquired skill. Even during the time John Jenkins attended Bates, some were questioning the benefits of a liberal arts degree. Graduates sometimes complained that their degree failed to prepare them for a competitive marketplace without additional post-graduate training. The traditional study of history, literature, writing, philosophy, sociology, psychology, and the creative arts was felt to be a relic of the past. Only later, years after graduation, do some students realize that their ability to make compelling arguments, communicate well, and problem solve have helped them stand out both in the workplace and as strong voices in their communities.

As John Jenkins settled into Maine, he ventured onto the ski slopes at Lost Valley, less than a 20-minute drive from the Bates campus. Offering a modest 231-foot vertical drop, the inexpensive day passes at Lost Valley attracted a steady stream of Bates students and young families from the surrounding communities.

The young man from Newark learned the basics of skiing: how to turn, snowplow, and stop. On his first day at Lost Valley, he desperately wanted to just let loose and experience the thrill of racing downhill, so when he reached the top, off he went pell-mell for the bottom. As he barreled down the mountain, unable to stop, he screamed, "Look out, look out!" before winding up in a snowbank, a white heap of snow nearly burying him completely. His face and beard were covered with snow, and he shouted, "Hey, now I look just like you guys!"

He was invited to join the Bates College modern dance group. As one of the few males in the ensemble, he often performed a series of lifts during the performances. Fellow dancer Geri Fitzgerald worried that with his enthusiasm and strength, lifting her into the air, she was going

John Jenkins kept close friendships with many of his Bates College classmates. In the top photo he joins Jill Bruce and Mel Donalson. In the bottom photo he's with Geri Fitzgerald, with whom he performed in the Bates College modern dance ensemble.

to be launched clear off the stage and into the audience. At campus dances, he would get so caught up in the music that he would suddenly drop into a full split on the floor and keep on dancing, never missing a beat.

Another friend, Jill Bruce, who maintained a more than 40-year friendship with Jenkins after graduation, remembers, "John was always center stage. The music would start up, you'd hear John yell, and the crowd would part like the Red Sea parted for Moses in *The Ten Commandments*. In 1975, the Jackson 5 introduced the Robot moves in their song, "Dancin' Machine." John took those moves and artfully incorporated karate into his "performance." As the pre-game music heated up the crowd for a wintry basketball contest at the Bates Alumni Gym, against rival Middlebury, it was Jenkins who led the Bates student body in a rendition of the hit song, "Kung Fu Fighting." He was, it would seem, everywhere on campus.

What was unusual for a Bates College student was Jenkins' growing connection to the Lewiston-Auburn community. When his track teammate Chuck Radis asked if he was interested in participating in a children's puppet show, he readily agreed. Radis wrote the play: *Detective Uncle Obadiah and the Pillowcase Bandit,* and the two drew on the talents of classmates to create the hand puppets and build a portable puppet theater. The production soon made its debut at a Lewiston Head Start Program with Jenkins, of course, in the lead role.

The show began with a Black detective puppet popping up on stage holding a magnifying glass as Radis and Jenkins crouched shoulder to shoulder behind the stage. "Has anyone seen the Pillowcase Monster?" Jenkins' voice boomed. A few children weakly called out, "No."

The Jenkins puppet exited slowly, stage right, and out popped Jenkins, dressed identically as the puppet, complete with a white beard. He wandered among the children, magnifying glass in hand, looking for clues. From behind the stage, the pillowcase bandit suddenly emerged, boasting that he was going to steal every pillowcase in Maine. "No one will ever get a good night sleep ever again," he snarled.

The children cried out, "Look! The Pillowcase Monster!" John slowly turned around but by then Chuck Radis had pulled the

Pillowcase Monster out of sight. Jenkins shrugged his shoulders and turned back to the audience, looking for clues.

The pillowcase bandit popped up again. This time the children shouted at the top of their lungs, "Look!! Look!!" Jenkins quickly turned, again, too late. Finally, he made his way back to the edge of the stage, disappeared, and the Uncle Obadiah puppet appeared. "Have *YOU* seen the pillowcase monster?" he asked. By this point, the children were delirious with excitement as the pillowcase bandit crept onstage behind Obadiah.

Of course, Detective Obadiah eventually captured the pillowcase bandit. The pillowcase bandit promised he would be good. Instead of handing him over to the police, Obadiah made him his assistant. Maine's first Black superhero detective had saved the day. Perhaps it was in that moment that Jenkins' magical connection with the Lewiston-Auburn community began.

Even after he returned to school, karate remained an anchor for John Jenkins. He progressed to a black belt and was hungry for high-level competition. Lewiston, Maine, would seem to be an unlikely outpost for a top-flight karate dojo, but the Golden Fist soon developed critical connections with world-class karate artists.

The Golden Fist dojo was a school within the Kenkojuku Association, a style of Shotokan karate founded by Tomosaburo Okano of Hachioji City in Japan. Okano, a 22-year-old kamikaze pilot in the waning months of World War II, survived when his mission was scrubbed at the last minute. During the American occupation of Japan following the war, Okano developed deep and lasting ties with GIs who were fascinated by the martial arts and became avid students. When the GIs returned to the U.S., they brought their interest in karate back to their hometowns and often opened schools. Later, top-level Japanese karate instructors such as Okano journeyed to the United States to live and teach karate.

An important Maine connection may have begun with Keiko Ingerson, owner of Keiko's Hair Care in Lewiston. Keiko, who had married an American GI, befriended Jenkins. As a native Japanese, she may have felt the same sense of isolation that Jenkins felt as a Black man in Lewiston. At one point, when money was tight, she temporarily offered Jenkins a room in her home, and the two remained friends for decades.

Keiko's connections extended to the international karate community, and she was close to both Tomosaburo Okano and Masakazu Takahashi, a student of Okano's. By then, Takahashi (fondly known as Takahash) had become one of the most famous Japanese fighters of his era. He traveled from New York City to visit with Keiko and her family in Lewiston and often taught at the Golden Fist. When Jenkins learned that another karate master, Toyotaro Miyazaki, the man he had read about in karate magazines since age 12, was coming to visit the Golden Fist, he was overjoyed. "I knew right away that five minutes with that guy would equal ten hours of training with anybody else."

"I started training with some of the best sensei, which allowed me to develop," Jenkins said. "You can have potential, but if you don't have good coaching, it's just potential. It became actual when I started getting good coaching." Roger Blais, already at the school, also remembers the transition at the Lewiston dojo. The newer techniques were characterized by deep, long stances that provided better stability and enabled powerful movements. The Shotokan style, with its offensive explosiveness and closed-fist fighting techniques, allowed fighters from the Golden Fist to compete more successfully in national competitions.

Another connection was Ren Halverson, who moved to Maine from New York and taught karate classes at the Boothbay YMCA. Jenkins met Halverson at a karate tournament in Portland. By coincidence, Halverson had also been a member of the Kenkojuku Association in New York, and the group became friends, often traveling together to karate tournaments. Before long Halverson was visiting and training at the Golden Fist as well.

Karate provided Jenkins a ready opportunity to hone his leadership and speaking skills. Halverson recalled one particularly impressive karate demonstration at Frederica Academy where his son, Eric, attended. "The entire school was present in the gym and filled the bleachers and chairs on the floor. Jenkins came out to a polite welcome from first graders through high school students. He set the tone by having them pat their thighs softly in unison, slowly at first, and then

John Jenkins with former Bates College football teammates Mel Donalson, top, and Ira J. Waldman.

building to a loud crescendo, then softer again. It sounded like rain. The kids totally loved it. They gave him a huge ovation even before he began his talk. I mean, the man captivated everyone without saying 20 words."

Halverson went on to add, "Then he began to speak and the entire school hung on every word. The theme was 'Don't hold yourself back by shooting low; think huge and put a system in place to attain your dream one goal at a time.' He emphasized the difference between a goal, which is attainable with hard work, and an ideal, which is not. Looking back, the karate demonstration was a huge hit, but it was John Jenkins' message that made the day so memorable for both the teachers and students. He was gracious, accommodating and funny, with real-life nuggets of wisdom for those who chose to grab them. When he was finished the standing ovation at my son's school lasted five minutes."

Fellow black-belt Roger Blais treasures a faded black-and-white photo he has kept of Jenkins demonstrating karate technique to another group of spectators. The photo shows eight karate students forming a line on the floor in front of a volunteer holding a wooden board. Jenkins is captured mid-air as he sprinted from one end of the gym and catapulted himself over the karate students, breaking the board with his leading foot.

Today, top Black martial arts practitioners in the United States are represented at every level of the sport, but in the late 1960s and 1970s when Jenkins began to compete, they were subject to both overt and subtle forms of discrimination. In martial arts tournaments in Southern California, for instance, they were often forced to compete against each other in the preliminary rounds, narrowing the field of opponents who would meet their Caucasian counterparts in the later rounds. The Black Karate Federation was founded in Los Angeles in response to perceived prejudice on the part of judges against Black competitors and exerted pressure on the sport to level the playing field. Steve Muhammad, a 10th degree black belt, co-founded the Black Karate Federation and became the organization's first president. He became one of the most dynamic and celebrated figures in the history of American martial arts.

In Maine tournaments, John Jenkins was often the only minority competing. As his reputation grew, the all-night out-of-state drives to tournaments became more and more frequent. Thankfully, neither Pam Wansker nor Ren Halverson can recall a match in which racial bias against Jenkins played a role.

One of Ren Halverson's favorite memories was a road trip to New York City to compete in a mixed martial arts tournament that drew hundreds of competitors from all over the East Coast. In John's initial match, he was paired against an NFL linebacker-sized fighter. They both traded reverse punches, but John's got home first, hitting the opponent's shoulder. A crack like a small-caliber shot reverberated in the ring; John's punch had dislocated the big guy's shoulder. End of match.

Later in the tournament, there was a huge free-for-all after an overzealous Kung Fu practitioner continued after the stop command. At one point, Halverson counted 59 competitors slugging it out in the middle of the gym. Referee Takahashi (a mentor to the Lewiston contingent) suddenly sprang into the melee and yelled STOP, sounding like a bullhorn . . . and everyone froze in their tracks. The tournament resumed

Years after he met Ren Halverson, left, at the Golden Fist dojo in Lewiston. John Jenkins officiated at the wedding of Ren and Cricket, who has since passed away.

after a dressing down by the tournament organizers, Mr. Miyazaki and Tomosaburo Okano.

The movie-set, dream-like quality of the tournament continued. At one point during a double Kama live-blade kata demonstration, a Mr. Hodiei from Florida cut his side deeply but never missed a beat in the form, finishing with a bloody gi to thunderous applause from the packed stands.

In the spring of 1975, when John Jenkins graduated from Bates College with a degree in psychology, he received a standing ovation. Those of us in the audience who rose and applauded felt a connection to him that was difficult to explain. In some undefinable way, he belonged to us all. His writings in the Bates student paper had laid bare both his academic and athletic struggles. His success in karate was well-known. He had stayed the course in college athletics even as he adjusted his expectations from stardom to a supportive role. His enthusiasm for new experiences was legendary—in his senior year he assisted in the development and production of a puppet play starring Uncle Obadiah (aka John Jenkins), exposing Head Start youngsters to a new phenomenon, a Black superhero detective.

According to one story, on graduation day, a meeting had been arranged for Jenkins to meet with civil rights activist Andrew Young, who gave the commencement address. Young was so impressed by Jenkins that he offered him a job in Georgia working in social justice. Jenkins politely declined: Maine was now his home.

By the time Jenkins graduated from Bates, the influence of the fledgling Afro-American Society was growing. The goal of increasing Black faculty and administrators was slowly being realized. His close friend, Mel Donalson, who had graduated several years before, returned to Lewiston after completing his M.A. in American Studies at the University of Iowa. That year, Donalson taught a class in African American Literature during the spring term at Bates. The course was widely praised. After a lengthy vetting process (he did not as yet have his PhD), he was hired to teach in the English Department in the fall of 1976.

In 1977, James Reese, a Black graduate from Middlebury College, joined the Bates administration. As of 2022, he continues his long association with the college as Associate Dean of Students for International

Student Programs. Another Black scholar and friend—Marcus Bruce was offered a job in admissions, strengthening the connection between Bates and Black applicants. Some years later, after receiving his doctorate at Yale University, Bruce returned to Bates where he later became a professor of Religious Studies and was the first awardee of the Benjamin E. Mays professorship. Doctor Mays' longstanding devotion to his alma mater was bearing fruit.

A Legacy in Karate

J enkins' dream of becoming a doctor was rekindled the summer after graduation. He signed up for a chemistry class through the University of Maine Augusta campus, and commuted 40 miles north in the evenings twice a week to Augusta for classes. Once again, although he was able to pass, he struggled with the course work. It was during this time that he covered his rent by working part-time

teaching pre-school in Head Start and as a cook at Graziano's restaurant in Lisbon while training and teaching at the Golden Fist. As one of his friends observed, he was becoming a true "Mainer." Cobbling together various jobs to eke out a living was the norm in a state which ranked low in economic opportunities.

He realized that he needed additional help to prepare himself for the all-important Medical College Entrance Test (MCAT) and met with Dr. Alvin F. Poussaint, the director of the Office of Recruitment and Multicultural Affairs at Harvard. Dr. Poussaint recommended that he continue his pre-medical studies at Columbia University in New York City, and assisted in making this a reality. Jenkins briefly moved to

John Jenkins practices basic karate stances—which are designed to give the practitioner a strong base—in front of the dramatic backdrop of the Grand Canyon.

midtown Manhattan, finding work as a DJ at a radio station, while he immersed himself, once again, in pre-medical classes.

After his pre-med classes ended in New York, he decided to sit for the MCATs (Medical College Entrance Exam) back in Maine. The day before the test, Pam Wansker, Mark Delaney, and sensei Masakazu Takahashi played doubles tennis with John. Mark hit a ball toward John that ricocheted off a post and shattered Jenkins' sunglasses, injuring his eye. He was seen in the local Emergency Room where his eye was flushed out and dilating drops applied. No permanent injury occurred, but the long-acting eye-drops made it difficult for him to read small print. Despite his eye injury, the next day he decided to go ahead with the test.

When John sat down for the MCAT, his vision was so blurred that he called the young African American woman preceptor over to help him fill out his name in the small boxes on the top line of the exam. She was horrified—since he wasn't wearing an eye patch, she didn't understand or believe that his blurred vision was due to a recent injury. After filling out his name and realizing the remainder of the test was in larger letters, he decided to take the rest of the test. Even so, the additional stress took away from his focus.

Remarkably, Jenkins was able to joke about what might have been the most important test of his life. Later that day, relaxing with his friends, he described the preceptor's reaction to his request for help: "Brother, are you sure you need help with this part? Are you sure you are supposed to be here?!" He was positive that she was totally embarrassed by his presence as an African American who had to ask for help with simply writing his name. Until his eye recovered, he teased his friend Mark Delaney mercilessly about the injury. For another week, he wore dark glasses and walked around tentatively, pretending to be blind. "Mark, Mark, buddy—are you still there?"

Despite his own inspirational message to youth groups to "think huge and put a system in place to attain your dream one goal at a time," and his emphasis that "the difference between a goal, which is attainable with hard work, and an ideal, which is not," his score on the all-important MCAT was not competitive. Not all goals can be fulfilled, but the discipline and focus he had developed in his pursuit of a career

As a karate instructor, John Jenkins emphasized not simply the skillful execution of martial arts techniques. He also melded portions of the Boy Scout oath he learned as a boy in Newark with traditional karate philosophy: "To help other people at all times; To keep myself physically strong, mentally awake, and morally straight."

in medicine fueled his desire to succeed on a larger stage. His failure to become a physician was, perhaps, his greatest lifetime disappointment.

As his dream of becoming a physician faded, John Jenkins' connection to the Lewiston-Auburn community deepened. When Richard Gates, the owner of the Golden Fist in Lewiston stepped down, Jenkins acquired the dojo and renamed it "The John Jenkins Golden Fist Karate Academy" offering "Special Personalized Instructions for women and men with emphasis on weight loss, self-defense, and physical conditioning for health."

He was now a black belt, and a year after graduating from Bates College, he won the AAU National Karate Championships. There, he caught the eye of Chuck Merriman, the head of the selection committee for the United States Karate Team, who invited him to try out for the national team. It was a life-changing connection.

Jenkins and Pam Wansker continued to date, living in separate apartments in Lewiston, and working out almost every day of the week at the Golden Fist. She vividly remembers one evening as they walked down Main Street in front of Central Maine General Hospital holding hands, and a man drove by in a car and rolled down the window. "Hey, N. . . ! Get your hands off that white woman!" John simply turned his head toward Pam and smiled sadly, "Baby, one of these days I'm going to be mayor of this city!"

In line with Jenkins' philosophy that the Golden Fist Karate Academy be more than a training ground for the martial arts, students were expected to be active members of the community. Reaching back to his years in the Boy Scouts in Newark, he melded portions of the Scout oath with traditional karate philosophy: "To help other people at all times; To keep myself physically strong, mentally awake, and morally straight."

The Dojo-Kun, an ethical guide for training in the martial arts and for behavior in everyday life, proudly hung on the wall of his studio where he and other instructors taught classes:

To strive for the perfection of character.
To follow the paths of truth.
To foster a spirit of effort.
To honor the principles of etiquette.
To guard against impetuous courage.

Reaching out to the community, the John Jenkins Golden Fist Karate Academy became a hub for food and clothing drives. Jenkins and his students gave karate demonstrations at local schools and businesses, and to senior citizens in retirement homes. John was one-part preacher, one part teacher in these early forays into the Lewiston-Auburn community. He was a charismatic speaker, often downplaying his own considerable abilities, while focusing on his message that karate was much more than breaking cement blocks.

As he honed his speaking abilities, he seemed to have an intuitive sense of how to connect with an audience that had rarely come in contact with a Black man. He bridged the gulf with self-deprecating humor, sometimes bordering on slapstick. The approach worked; by the time his students performed their carefully choreographed kata in unison, the audience was relaxed and focused. Over time, he was turning the Lewiston-Auburn region into a karate hotbed.

The year 1977 was a landmark year for Jenkins in the martial arts. He won the Mr. Maine Physique Contest and the Maine State Weapon Championship, even as he taught at his karate academy and competed across the country. He was named to the National AAU Karate Team to compete in Tokyo, Japan, in the World Karate Championships in Karate-do. In a *Lewiston Evening Journal* article written shortly after he was named to the national team, he explained how he qualified to be on the "A" team. "Because of the toughness of the competition, numerous accidental injuries resulted, including broken noses, ribs and fingers. The list of team hopefuls shortened rapidly as competitors dropped like flies."

Soon, he had waded through enough of the competition without injury to land a spot on the "A" team. "The key is that I survived without injury," Jenkins chuckled. "I was very lucky because I was fighting for my life."

His friend Ren Halverson remembers the lead-up to the World Championships when he would visit Jenkins in Lewiston. "On certain days he'd do short sprints, on other days he'd do distance runs to bolster endurance. On distance days, he'd do 10 miles, one mile backward for his calves. I went once (with him) on one of those days and I passed out after 5 miles, with him about 1,000 yards ahead. I hitchhiked back to the dojo where he was stretching before sparring practice. There were several of us, including a local professional boxer, who would take turns sparring with him. Rounds were 3 minutes and full tilt. He would jog in place for 1 minute before the next round. Nonstop for JJ. We went hard and fast because that's how the Japanese tournaments were run. When you squared off with him as a training partner you better bring your A game. He had superb control. The leg drive from those thighs of his reminded one of a thoroughbred breaking out of the starting gate. When he hit you, there were consequences that Newton described as equal and opposite reactions."

His preparations complete, he was dropped off at Logan Airport in Boston during the Christmas holidays for the long flight to Japan. There, he found the perfect gift for his sensei, Tomosaburo Okano, whom he hoped to visit after the competition in Japan: a cowboy hat.

As one of seven U.S. athletes picked for the World Championships, Jenkins knew he had to excel in both phases of Karate-Do competition; Kata and Kumite. There is no opponent in the Kata phase of Karate-Do. Similar to the compulsory routines in figure skating, competitors are judged on coordination, grace, and form. The Kumite, or fighting phase, can be compared to the sport of fencing—with consequences. Beneath their loose-fitting karategi, opponents wear protective gear for the groin, but little else. Points are scored for striking "vital" areas of the opponent's body. Closed hands and feet are utilized as offensive weapons. Significant injuries are common.

The American team was extraordinarily successful in the Tokyo karate-do championships. About 260 athletes from 32 countries took part in the second World Championships and the U.S. team did not have the prestige or track record of the Japanese or other powerhouses such as France, Spain, or the Netherlands. Before the World Championships, sensei Okano invited Jenkins to a special dinner. He poured a glass of sake for Jenkins and went on in his conversation with others at the table. Jenkins waited for a signal from the sensei before drinking the sake. None came. At the end of the dinner, Okano stood and bowed to Jenkins. He was proud that his student had not taken a sip of the sake; he was in training. When American Domingo Llanos was ill on the day of the kata competition and coach Chuck Merriman needed a replacement, he saw that John was more than ready, helping the U.S. team to a

John Jenkins stands with his 1st Place trophy at the 1985 World Karate/Jiu-Jitsu Championship in Trinidad.

surprising third place in the Kata competition and fifth spot in Kumite. Jenkins' performance earned him membership in the All-Japan Karate Black Belt Association.

Jenkins stayed several additional weeks in Japan at the invitation of Grand Master Tomosaburo Okano. In a follow-up *Lewiston Sun Journal* interview when he returned to the States, Jenkins recalled his time with Okano: "I learned a lot from him, and he also introduced me to many of his friends and city officials."

His friend Ren Halverson has a more vivid recollection of John Jenkins' time in Japan with Master Okano. "Mr. Okano brought him to a mountain ledge and stood with his back to open space at the edge of the ledge. A couple hundred feet below were rocks. No place to go but down. He told John to attack him. When John told me the story, it was hilarious to hear John's reaction to the command, but he followed the instructions. Without moving his feet Okano shifted his body sideways, slipping the punch and then caught John by the back of his gi to counter his forward momentum, saving him from falling off the cliff.

Then Okano said, 'OK, switch places.' Of course, in the telling of the story, John mimicked looking over his shoulder and flailing his arms at the edge of the cliff, but he had complete trust in Okano's ability and dutifully followed the instructions. He survived the encounter with newfound confidence in both his offensive and defensive abilities.

Halverson remembers that following the lesson, Jenkins said, "When you get 100 percent real with training at this level, it transcends getting caught up in a mental banter inside your own mind. Death can be a serious teacher." When they returned to Okano's home, Okano told him that in facing critical life experiences, there are opportunities to use techniques like tai sabaki ("whole body movement," or repositioning.). It was not merely a physical maneuver, but could be applied to interactions in daily life. Before Jenkins left Japan, he was awarded a higher degree black belt by sensei Okano.

Over time, Jenkins' favorite move in karate came to be tai sabaki—to evade attack at the last possible moment. It placed the attacker in a disadvantageous position and allowed a clean, balanced and pure counter-attack opportunity. Halverson believed Jenkins used tai sabaki frequently in business and politics as well. One can imagine scenarios where his openness and sense of humor had invited his adversaries in politics to underestimate him. Perhaps, they let down their guard and unknowingly revealed more than they intended. At a certain point in a meeting, John would verbally reposition himself, catching his opponent off-guard and thus gain a political edge.

The year 1977 was also successful for John Jenkins as a coach. Under his tutelage, Pam Wansker had earned her brown belt and competed in karate competitions with Jenkins and other students from the Golden Fist. At the AAU National Karate Championships—the same competition Jenkins used as a springboard for the World Championships in Japan—she competed in a round-robin preliminary tournament, the winner earning a place in the championship rounds. She won her first bout, and then her second and third. Before she knew it, she was fighting in the women's advanced black belt kumite AAU finals.

When she won the championship, an Associated Press interviewer asked, "Didn't you feel like you didn't belong?" Wansker replied, "In most of the other bouts, I was competing against women with black belts, but facing a brown belt in the finals shows you how much a black belt means."

Ironically, and with John Jenkins' encouragement, it was Pam Wansker who would become a physician. "He pointed out that I had decent grades and all the prerequisites, and he essentially talked me into applying." In the fall of 1977, she moved to the Midwest and began her freshman year at the Kansas City College of Osteopathic Medicine. Four years later, she returned to Maine for her family practice residency before setting up an office in Greene, about 40 minutes north of Lewiston, where she remains today. The rigors of medical school and time and distance eventually led to the breakup of their relationship, but the two remained friends.

By the time he arrived home after the World Championships in Japan, Jenkins had become the most recognizable face in the twin cities of Lewiston-Auburn, and he delighted in the attention. His students at the Golden Fist Karate Academy on Pine Street performed at nursing homes, local school gymnasiums, the American Legion, Kora, YWCA, and the Fraternal Order of Eagles. They traveled to Women's Clubs and the Elks, Rotary, and Knights of Columbus. Leading them in their kata and explaining the finer points of karate to his primarily Franco-American audience, Jenkins mixed lessons in humility and discipline with humor and slapstick. Like all great story tellers and preachers, he radiated the "it" factor his cousin Francella Trueblood first recognized from their days growing up in Newark. School children at his performances idolized Jenkins. Years later, as adults, they would often stop by to chat when Jenkins ate at local restaurants (he preferred buffets—the man had a legendary appetite), to shake his hand and let him know the effect his words had on them during a critical period of their lives.

5

PepTalk and Political Success

When asked why he made Lewiston-Auburn his home after graduating from Bates College, Jenkins replied, "A Bates College education is what brought me to Maine. Work and quality of life are what kept me in Maine. The alternative was to go back to Newark to stand in long unemployment lines."

In the same interview, he was asked, "So then how—or why—has the community embraced you the way it has?" Jenkins replied, "Many residents (in Lewiston) are practicing Catholics. Historically, Maine had one of the first African American Catholic bishops in the nation." Then, drawing parallels between the Franco-American experience and growing up on the streets of Newark, New Jersey, he said, "When I toured a vacant mill building, an elderly former mill worker said to me, 'I remember when the trains would arrive and this room was filled from floor to ceiling with bales of cotton to be woven into textiles. Your

(Russ Dillingham/Lewiston Sun Journal)

people (Black Americans) were held to pick the cotton, and my people (Franco Americans) were held to weave the cotton. Both peoples—both white and Black—were held captive in the textile industry.'"

Even if her analogy paled beside the far more brutal reality of Black slavery, Jenkins graciously understood the attempt by the Franco-American woman to see parallels in their struggles to overcome discrimination. It was a lesson in cultural accommodation he would never forget. Years later he commented, "In some respects, maybe the Franco-American and African American histories aren't too far apart. Labor in the mills was just brutal. You had to have some strong resolve to just survive in those kinds of work conditions."

But now, he had to make a living. Graduates from Bates often complained that their liberal arts degree prepared them poorly for the job market. Following Bates, they entered medical school or law school, or obtained advanced degrees in social work, psychology, or teaching. Banking and the insurance industry valued their wide knowledge base and ability to problem solve.

John Jenkins knew how to relate to people from all walks of life. He was a skillful storyteller and mimic who used humor to set people at ease. *(Russ Dillingham/Lewiston Sun Journal)*

Although he was a celebrity in Lewiston-Auburn, an AAU National Karate Champion, and a key member of the U.S. Karate Team at the recent World Karate Championships, his income from the Golden Fist Karate Academy barely covered his rent and living expenses. When he finally had enough money to purchase a car, he bought a compact green sedan. He was grateful not to depend on others to travel to karate tournaments, and he took great pride in car ownership. Additional financial stability arrived when Bates College offered him a job as director of housing in 1980.

He continued to dream. After his success at the World Karate championships, Jenkins developed a business built on his love of public speaking and the goal setting and discipline of karate. As the founder and president of PepTalk, he found a ready market for his inspirational talks through his growing connections in Lewiston/Auburn. Many of the same businesses and nonprofit organizations where his karate students had performed were interested in Jenkins' message of personal and organizational growth. And PepTalk helped pay the bills.

Casting a wide net, Jenkins wrote in a brochure:

> At PepTalk.com we are excited to offer tailored all-occasion seminars in-person and on-line. Live chats, video archives, and PepTalk merchandise available. We offer all-occasion Seminars, Services, and Special Projects, including age, ability, and culturally appropriate tailored seminars. Professional services include, but are not limited to, insurance, real estate, notary, and organizational development. Special projects are welcomed.

Over time, PepTalk motivational talks expanded into seminars on health, drug prevention, and literacy. His reach expanded beyond Maine, and eventually reached overseas with seminars in China and Japan. With the advent of the internet, organizations could learn more about PepTalk at PepTalk.com. Over the next 30 years, his zeal for new motivational projects never dulled. He became president of HealthKick USA.com and founded READ ME, a family literacy project.

Equal parts storyteller, preacher, and Black superhero, he could be outrageously funny. Lewiston friend Donna Card remembers inviting

When Things Fall Apart

We Stand Together

"Although our journeys started in different places, we have always been on the same path. This path has led us to be an integral part of the United States (**US**). In the final analysis, there is no 'we' and 'them', there is only **US**."-Honorable John Jenkins

her former karate mentor to her fitness salon to discuss personal safety and self-defense with a group of 15 women dressed in leotards and tights. Jenkins arrived in his form-fitting track suit and began his presentation by asking the women what their concerns were.

There had been a recent mugging near the fitness studio, and the women fidgeted, uncomfortable with admitting they felt unsafe going to the evening class. John sensed that he needed to lighten up the session and went for a visual knockout. He noticed a large purse on the floor next to one of the women, and asked in a silky, velvet, voice: "Maam, may I borrow your purse?" Lifting it up, he groaned, "Whoa, whatch'yall got in this thing? Honey, you don't need me to teach you anything, just swing this thing at someone and you'll knock 'em out cold!"

Now they were all laughing. He hooked the bag on his shoulder and strutted on his tip-toes as if he was in heels, playing it, pretending to use a compact and put on lipstick. By now, the women were in stitches. He asked for a volunteer from the audience. One woman pointed to Card and said, "She invited you here. Pick her! Pick her!"

Card continued the story. "He looked at me and wiggled his eyebrows. 'Oh, shit, I thought to myself, I'm supposed to be the attacker.' Well, let it suffice to say that we all laughed nonstop for the next 45 minutes while I tried to grab his purse, attack him from behind, kick him in the groin—only to get air and baggy pants—while he is wailing and screaming for help, to the point that I simply fell down laughing and crying, holding my sides.

"Once we all managed to stop laughing, he got serious and explained how to try and get out of a chokehold, how to look at a dark parking lot differently, how to carry your keys in a defensive way, and so much more. Those women left that night feeling empowered and educated and had *so* much fun in the process. I heard about it for years, (seriously, *years* later!) from women saying how informative and empowering it had been, and what a wonderful guy he was. I even had one woman's husband, who worked out of state, tell me that he felt better about his wife being alone so often, because she felt less afraid."

In 1992, John Jenkins was approached by friends to run for mayor of Lewiston. Up until that time, he hadn't considered running for

Empowerment was the overarching lesson of John Jenkins' PepTalk presentations. *(Russ Dillingham/Lewiston Sun Journal)*

political office. Jenkins must have been flattered, but did not immediately agree to run. Between his job as director of housing at Bates, operating the Golden Fist Karate Academy, and his income from PepTalk, at age 40, he had finally cobbled together a good living. His supporters persisted; as a small business owner, who better understood the concerns of everyday voters struggling to make ends meet?

Jenkins agreed to run and won the election by a three-to-one margin. It helped that Franco-Americans, who comprised the majority of voters, viewed him as one of their own. Many recalled Jenkins' friendship with Franco-Americans while working at the Bates College cafeteria, and through his karate demonstrations at various social clubs and nursing homes. For most Lewiston residents, the fact that he was Black seemed to be irrelevant.

Jenkins' win mirrored another successful African American campaign in nearby Augusta where William Burney became mayor in 1988. As the first Black mayor in northern New England, Burney held the post for four consecutive two-year terms, and presided over a period of steady economic growth in Augusta. Elwood Watson, an assistant professor of American history at East Tennessee State University interviewed Jenkins extensively for a paper he wrote for Maine History in 2001 entitled, "William Burney and John Jenkins: A Tale of Maine's Two African American Mayors." The parallels between the two men were significant. Both men had attended Maine schools; Jenkins graduating from Bates College, Burney from the University of Maine School of Law. A key to their successful campaigns was their ability to develop close friendships across racial lines in college and later in their local communities.

"Whether John was talking to you one on one or as part of a crowd, he had a way of making you feel as if you were the most important person in the world at that moment," remembered Rick Denison, who worked at Bates College for many years. "He and I were tablemates once at a formal dinner. At the start, I was the only person there who knew him. By the end, everyone at that table felt as if John were a lifelong friend. That's the effect he had on people."

Bates College football teammate Bob Littlefield's prescient words uttered more than 20 years earlier—when he described Jenkins as "the Mayor of Bates College" had taken on new meaning. The honorary Mayor of Bates was now the Mayor of Maine's second-largest city.

John Jenkins took his responsibilities as mayor of Lewiston very seriously. Although the Lewiston city charter limited the power of the mayor, Jenkins' ability to persuade and engage were invaluable in jump starting a number of projects. He was the city's greatest cheerleader. *(Russ Dillingham / Lewiston Sun Journal)*

When Jenkins assumed the mayorship in 1993, Lewiston's textile mills had long been closed, its downtown marred by dilapidated buildings and empty storefronts. The loss of jobs had triggered a decline in Lewiston's population to about 36,000 from more than 41,000 in its manufacturing prime. Young people were abandoning the city for jobs in Portland or were leaving the state entirely.

Although the Lewiston city charter limited the power of the mayor, Jenkins' ability to persuade and engage were invaluable in jump starting a number of projects. He was the city's greatest cheerleader. Among Jenkins' major accomplishments as mayor (particularly in the eyes of Franco-Americans) was his success in attracting the Forum Francophone Des Affairs, an international trade organization, to Lewiston. Lewiston was picked as the national headquarters for the 45-country French-speaking coalition. He arranged a meeting with the South African Ambassador to the United States to improve the region's business and cultural relationship with South Africa. The symbolism of this gesture was clear: A Black mayor could be good for business now that South Africa had recently abandoned its policy of apartheid.

As a limited-government but growth-oriented Democrat of the Edmund Muskie mold, Jenkins' administration developed and implemented Maine's first cap on city spending, the "Coltrap Amendment," limiting growth of government to no more than the Consumer Price Index. Jenkins described the Coltrap Amendment as "an opportunity to have government, much like citizens, live within its means at an approximately 3 percent growth rate."

Jenkins won a second term as mayor of Lewiston in 1995 by another landslide. By then, the Androscoggin River separating Lewiston and Auburn, although far from pristine, was no longer a dumping ground for untreated waste from upstream paper mills and tanneries. The Twin Cities were undergoing a minor renaissance. Businesses were opening and the tax base expanding. After years of unpaid taxes by the Bates Mill, the city had taken possession of the mill on Canal Street and the site would soon be an incubator for entrepreneurs. Jenkins established a closer relationship with neighboring Auburn in order to cut down on duplicate expenses and improve services. He reached out to young people and made them feel that they were a part of the city's political structure.

Although a Democrat, John Jenkins made a point of seeking common ground with Republicans as well as those with more conservative views. He demonstrated those qualities while serving as Lewiston's mayor, as well as during his time as state senator, comfortably sharing the stage with Republican Sens. Bob Dole and Bill Cohen and Olympia Snowe during Lewiston's bicentennial celebration. *(Russ Dillingham / Lewiston Sun Journal)*

In 1995, Jenkins turned the Golden Fist Academy over to several former students. He was getting deeper into the political world and found it difficult to manage both PepTalk and his karate business. He was dating Ann Parker, a local real estate agent, originally from Aroostook County to the north. The two had been friends since the mid-1970s but were now a couple. Ann understood Jenkins' private side. They had a small group of interracial friends with whom they could relax and enjoy each other's company. She was an excellent cook, and Jenkins had a legendary appetite. Eventually, the two became engaged.

The year 1995 was also the 30th anniversary of the Lewiston Armory Muhammad Ali–Sonny Liston Championship fight where Ali dropped Liston less than two minutes into the first round. The "mystery punch" became part of boxing lore and briefly landed Lewiston in the national news. Jenkins, with an eye for favorable publicity, hoped to entice Ali back to Lewiston on the 30th anniversary of the fight. There would be a dinner celebration and, later, Ali would attend a boxing match at the Armory. Unexpectedly, Muhammad Ali accepted.

According to a *New York Times* article, when Jenkins tried to convince Ali to come to Lewiston for the 30th anniversary of the 1965 fight, he may have exaggerated when he said, "Here came Ali, at the dawn of the Civil Rights era, a different kind of Black man, who wouldn't let others define him and who was threatening to a whole lot of white folks. It was Lewiston that gave him a chance to defend his title and go from there to become the most famous person in the world."

Never mind that Ali had been roundly booed when he entered the ring against Liston in 1965, or that the *Lewiston Sun* had referred to him as Cassius Clay rather than his adopted Muslim name of Muhammed Ali; it was Lewiston that agreed to put on the match when the rest of the country refused to sanction the fight.

Even after Ali had agreed to come to Lewiston for the 30th anniversary of his famous fight, the plans for the event nearly came crashing down. Days before Ali's arrival, the money for Ali's appearance fee was frustratingly short. Jenkins turned to his friend, Billy Johnson, a Lewiston real estate developer and fight fan. The two turned to friends in the community, emphasizing the positive publicity for Lewiston having

IN 1995, as mayor of Lewiston, John Jenkins reached out to Muhammad Ali with an invitation to come to the city on the 30th anniversary of the Lewiston Armory Muhammad Ali–Sonny Liston Championship fight in 1965 where Ali dropped Liston less than two minutes into the first round. To his surprise, Muhammad Ali accepted . . . and demonstrated, during the visit, that he was still the Champ, in more than just a boxing ring. *(Courtesy of Billy Johnson)*

the former champ return to Lewiston. The good will of Jenkins and the persistence of Billy Johnson averted a major disappointment for the city.

The next evening, Ali's entourage arrived in a white limousine at the Ramada Inn in Lewiston. Floyd Patterson, another former heavyweight champ, was there. So was a security contingent, a nurse, and Ali's brother to smooth out the details. When Ali was introduced to Mayor John Jenkins, he was taken aback by Jenkins' skin color and cracked, "How the hell did you get here?"

Steve Cherlock, in his *Lewiston Sun Journal* article described what came next: (Ali's) wit was on display during the banquet. Lewiston did not have a Key to the City to hand out to dignitaries. The best Jenkins could find was a city lapel pin. "I handed him the pin," Jenkins said. Ali looked at the pin. He looked at me. Then he looked at the audience. In true Ali fashion—the timing was perfect—he said, 'I came all the way here to Maine for this pin'—(while) holding this little pin in his very large hand. Everyone broke out laughing." Trying to recover, Jenkins apologized with a smile and then said the city did not give out keys because keys symbolized locked doors, which got Ali laughing.

Following the dinner, Ali—who was already in the early stages of Parkinson's disease—retired to his hotel room to rest before his entrance as the celebrity guest for the fight at the Armory. Billy Johnson realized that this was his chance to meet Ali and asked Jenkins if he could help him meet the champ. The two took the elevator to Ali's floor and were met immediately by several members of the security detail. They remembered Mayor Jenkins, (who could forget John Jenkins?), but the little white guy? Who the hell was he?

There was an awkward silence before Jenkins said, "This is my bodyguard."

The two security guards scrutinized Billy Johnson—who was significantly shorter than Jenkins—and then turned their attention back to Jenkins. "Your bodyguard?"

"My bodyguard," Jenkins repeated with a straight face. Billy Johnson stared straight ahead, this close to meeting his childhood hero.

One guard looked at his watch. "The champ must be getting up about now. Let me go check."

He disappeared into a suite down the hall and a moment later motioned Jenkins and Billy Johnson inside. Muhammed Ali was sitting on the couch, his nurse hovering nearby, and he motioned the two to take a seat. Ali chatted with Jenkins for a few minutes before Jenkins said, "My friend here, Billy Johnson, has a question to ask you." Ali shifted his attention to Johnson.

"We have a good friend, Tom Callahan, who's dying of ALS," Johnson began. "He's weak as a kitten and getting close to the end. His wife is fighting to keep him at home. Big fight fan. You're his hero. His house is on the way to the Armory; we have time to stop there on our way to the fight." Billy paused, "Will you go? It would mean the world to him."

Ali nodded he would go and extended his hand to Billy. It was well past dark by then. Johnson and Jenkins drove one car and the white limo, filled with Ali's people, followed close behind. Billy Johnson pulled into a side street near the Armory. The champ led the group up the front steps of a modest house, an umbrella shielding him from

At the request of Billy Johnson, Muhammad Ali paid a surprise visit to a friend, Tom Callahan, "a big fight fan" who was dying of ALS, sometimes referred to as Lou Gehrig's disease. *(Courtesy of Billy Johnson)*

the steady drizzle. Inside the living room was Callahan resting in his favorite brown leather easy chair, a tracheotomy tube coursing out of his neck and connecting to an oxygen tank on the side table. ALS had advanced to the point where he barely had strength enough to breathe. His arms and legs were atrophied and weak. If you looked closely at his forearms, you would see fasciculations—a worm-like quivering of the muscles—where the nerve connections to the muscles were barely functional. In a few more months, Tommy Callahan would be gone.

The pictures Billy Johnson took during the brief visit tell it all: Callahan's absolute shock at seeing Muhammed Ali quietly entering his living room, the grace of Ali as he extended his massive hand to greet Callahan, Ali lifting up Callahan to a standing position like a rag doll and posing for a group photo with Tom and Mrs. Callahan, and former champ Floyd Patterson, who once said, "They said I was the fighter who got knocked down the most, but I also got up the most."

In the final photo, John Jenkins is in the foreground, his eyes sparkling, a smile of pure delight spreading across his face. Callahan is barely standing, one arm around his wife, the other behind the back of Ali. Billy Johnson, who took the photo, remembers that Ali, whose left

The champ graciously agreed, extending his hand to greet Callahan and posing for several pictures before heading to the Lewiston Armory for the evening's festivities. *(Courtesy of Billy Johnson)*

arm is hidden behind Callahan, was actually holding Callahan up by his belt. Moments later, Callahan collapsed back into his easy chair like he'd gone 10 rounds. With practiced hands, Tommy's wife connected the oxygen tube back to the tracheotomy. It was time to leave.

Later that night, the Armory was packed for the heavyweight bout. The national press picked up the story of Lewiston's first African American mayor and Muhammed Ali sitting together at ringside, looking over photos of the 1965 fight. The success of the 1995 celebration paved the way for another commemoration in 2015 on the 50th anniversary of the bout. Lewiston native Charlie Hewitt produced the documentary, "Raising Ali," as a metaphor for the city's ongoing fight for economic and social progress. Hewitt described the film as "a sentimental portrait of a struggling old factory town that was visited by greatness."

But it was on that rainy night in the living room of Tommy Callahan where the story began, a moment of pure, loving humanity between Blacks and whites, when Lewiston opened itself to the gathering forces of American social change, embodied by Muhammed Ali.

Billy Johnson treasures the iconic photo of Ali looming over the prostrate Sonny Liston less than two minutes into that long ago 1965

Muhammad Ali looks over photos of his 1965 heavyweight fight against Sonny Liston as John Jenkins and others look on. *(Courtesy of Billy Johnson)*

fight in Lewiston, Maine. Ali's fist is cocked and he's ready to brawl. Those close to the action heard Ali say, "Get up and fight, sucker!" Thirty years later, Lewiston was pulling itself to its feet and fighting back.

Jenkins' influence now extended beyond Lewiston. He was mentioned in a *Newsweek* magazine article on rising Black politicians and his PepTalk presentations were in demand. He received a National TRIO award in recognition of his inspirational work with individuals from disadvantaged backgrounds. He was named to a U.S. Department of Labor Glass Ceiling Commission to study the problem of barriers to advancement in employment faced by women and minority workers, and to recommend ways to remove those barriers.

Jenkins served the public and governed based on the principles he had learned in the martial arts. He realized that even in politics, mutual understanding and respect provided a foundation to work through contentious issues. "There are rules of engagement," Jenkins later said. "Just as we cross swords in fencing, people can sometimes cross words. How do you engage in a sensible way? There's a way to engage and disengage. It's really a strategy of life. How do you disagree without becoming disagreeable? How do you contend without being contentious? These are the underpinnings that add to the social fabric that we call community. These are the things I learned and live by and have served me well."

Jenkins' ability to coalesce support in the Lewiston community may have played a role in the decision of former Dean of Bates College James Carignan, a few years later, to run successfully for Lewiston City Council. Bates had traditionally been insulated from the economic decline of the Twin Cities, and few Bates students stayed in the area following graduation. Carignan believed that colleges like Bates had a responsibility to educate students in good citizenship. In his role as city councilor, Carignan lived this belief, contributing toward the revitalization and economic success of his community.

Jenkins and Carignan laid the groundwork for a more collaborative and mutually beneficial relationship between Bates College and the Lewiston-Auburn region. Eventually, this relationship was formalized with the opening of the Harwood Center on the Bates campus, whose

President Bill Clinton greets John Jenkins during a visit to the White House.

mission is to "weave the resources and concerns of our community into the Bates educational experience and onto the Bates campus."

Midway through his second two-year term as mayor of Lewiston, John Jenkins was encouraged by Maine Democrats to run for a seat in the State Senate. His popularity was at an all-time high, but money was tight; he no longer worked at Bates College as director of housing. He accepted the offer and beat an incumbent Republican in the election, becoming the first Black state senator in Maine history. This election, however, was filled with personal attacks and racial overtones.

Balancing the demands of mayor of Lewiston and state senator was only possible because Maine's Legislature was (theoretically) a part-time position. State senators and members of the House often continued in their jobs as farmers and small-business owners, nurses and teachers, as they considered hundreds of bills and passed a biannual state budget. But the part-time nature of serving in the Maine Legislature was deceptive; senators served on committees, attended legislative debates, and responded to lobbyists and constituents' concerns year-round. And the pay, at less than $10,000, was more of an honorarium than an actual salary.

Now that Jenkins no longer operated the karate dojo, he needed another source of income besides PepTalk. Fortunately, UNUM Insurance Co. offered him a position as its director of multicultural marketing and business development. The job required considerable travel on behalf of the company. Within a few months, however, the freshman senator was overwhelmed. Between meetings with UNUM clients and his responsibilities as mayor of Lewiston, he missed a number of committee meetings and votes at the State House.

Overwhelmed, he approached the Democratic political leadership to resign his Senate seat but was convinced to stay on; his vote was needed in the nearly evenly divided Democratic and Republican body. Some of his fellow Democrats were frustrated with Jenkins and challenged his attendance record, not realizing the economic bind Jenkins was in. Another surprise was his interest in exploring compromises with Republicans across the aisle. Although Jenkins was a social liberal, he had earned the respect of voters in Lewiston with his fiscally conservative leanings. At the end of his term as state senator, he did not run again.

John Jenkins celebrates with supporters his election to the Maine Senate in 1996. He ran as a Democrat and retained his position as Lewiston's mayor. *(Russ Dillingham / Lewiston Sun Journal)*

By some measures, his two years in the Senate were not as successful as his years as mayor of Lewiston. Although he connected with fellow state senators on an individual level, he silently chafed at voting for Democratic initiatives which he thought were unnecessary or overly expensive. His displeasure (and perhaps impatience) with being a foot soldier in the Democratic Party may have held him back from forming the necessary connections for later success in statewide politics.

In retrospect, he could have resigned as mayor of Lewiston and focused on the Senate, but this would have meant trading in the high-profile but largely ceremonial position of mayor for the relative anonymity of the Legislature where his voice was one of many. Lewiston was his home and where his real interest resided. In a later interview with Joshua Shea at the *Lewiston-Auburn* magazine, looking back at his time serving simultaneously as both mayor and state senator, he was asked, "And nobody complained about your mayoral attendance record?" Jenkins replied, "My attendance record as mayor of Lewiston was 100 percent."

But the experience of serving in the Senate was invaluable in many respects. While he shared many of the Democratic Party's priorities, particularly on social policy, he leaned toward a fiscally conservative view. At times, this put him at odds with party leadership, particularly on bills which could contribute to higher taxes. As mayor of a community which was economically depressed, he knew the value of governing with fiscal restraint. As an individual, he had always struggled to make ends meet.

Another factor in his disillusionment with the two-party system was the outsized importance that money played in a candidate's viability in statewide elections. He had reservations about whether he was willing to play the money game in order to run for future elections. In a state where James Longley had already won the governorship as an Independent in 1975, Jenkins saw that Mainers did not reject a candidate out of hand who worked outside of the established two-party system. Indeed, it could be an advantage to run as a perpetual outsider.

Following his term as state senator, Jenkins refocused on his Pep-Talk business. By then, he was no longer working for the UNUM Insurance Co. as its director of multicultural marketing and business development. He was seemingly everywhere, traversing the state from Fort Kent to Kittery, from Jackman to Boothbay Harbor, providing seminars and keynote addresses to small groups and businesses, schools and clubs. His talks focused on character, ethics, and hard work. Although Jenkins attributed his own development to the lessons he learned in karate and the Boy Scouts, he understood that there were many paths leading to a full and meaningful life.

As a speaker, he was a work of art. Taking a cue from the Baptist preachers he had grown up listening to at his mother's Baptist church, he often repeated key phrases when he wanted to drive home a particular message. He never read from notes. His voice ranged from a soft whisper to a bellowing call to action. And interspersed with it all were self-deprecating moments of comic relief, complete with over-the-top sequences when he would assume two personalities in a hilarious conversation with himself.

Jenkins was a master at having the audience join in his antics, pleading with them, cajoling them, getting grown men and women to shout a particularly uplifting phrase. He borrowed from the Bible. He borrowed from Abraham Lincoln, Martin Luther King Jr., and comedian Bill Cosby. His gift was to meld an audience of individuals into a collective voice. By the time he honed in on his central message, the audience was totally engaged.

As the keynote speaker on a YouTube video for the Think Local Community Network, viewers can watch Jenkins in full-on mode. He begins by thanking Jeffrey, the man who introduced him, and asks the audience to give him a round of applause. "But also," he continues while clapping, "let's give a round of applause to everyone in this room. Thank you! Because you're the ones in this room who make our communities work. Give yourself a hand. Thank you. Thank you!"

In less than a minute, the audience was whistling and clapping, completely under his spell.

By the time he moved into the body of his speech, the crowd was feeling the spirit like an old-time revival meeting. He introduced the acronym (Jenkins loved acronyms) LEVER to describe the work that the Think Local Community Network performs. "Lever sounds like lead, and L is for lead. You Lead by example! You LEAD by example. Now repeat after me and move your arm up and down. That's it, up and down, I am a lever. The E in the word LEVER is for ethics because you are ethically bound to deliver prompt, trustworthy products and services."

A tall man with a black beard stopped on his way out the door, paused, turned back, and grinned. "V is about value and validating," Jenkins continued. "You are providing a service to your communities. That's what makes communities work. The second E is about enthusiasm! Passion! You are fired up about your business. It's contagious. You're taking that passion and turning it into a paycheck. You need both: Passion, and a paycheck. One more time, I'm a LEVER!"

The man at the door was really into it now. He was moving his arm up and down like he was pumping water from a well. "And lastly, the R in lever, that's for restraint. Never forget your core business. It's good to go after new opportunities, but there were people standing by your side who believed in you when you began. Show them the love. One more time, "I'm a LEVER, because LEVERs . . . ," Jenkins paused and opened wide that high-wattage smile, "become B-E-L-I-E-V-E-R-S. Thank you! Thank you very much!"

There's no question that John Jenkins was hugely entertaining. Whether his uplifting presentations catalyzed long-term change in his audiences or not is an open question. Ren Halverson, who often trained with Jenkins at the Lewiston dojo, believes his impact in karate was life-changing for his students. Many of the boys and girls who enrolled in classes at the dojo came from the streets of Lewiston. At age 12 or 13 they were already hardened young adults, often attracted to karate

John Jenkins and his fiancee Ann Parker. Whenever they went out dining together, Parker recalls they were frequently approached by people wanting to shake Jenkins' hand or share a story about his impact. *(Russ Dillingham / Lewiston Sun Journal)*

by the promise of learning to deliver a good butt-kicking. Sensei Jenkins turned their expectations around, combining the discipline of the martial arts with lessons in humility and service. Not every student absorbed these lessons, but for those who did, the trajectory of their lives was forever altered.

Ann Parker frequently went out to dinner with Jenkins at local restaurants. She recalls strangers shyly approaching their table and wanting to shake his hand. They recalled the day they heard his motivational message, where they were standing, who they were with, and who they had become afterward.

It pleased Jenkins to know that he was making a difference in people's lives. He remembered one time when he had been invited to speak in Michigan at the Interlochen Center for the Arts by a man who had heard him speak at Bridgton Academy decades before. "He told me that . . . as a student at Bridgton Academy, while trying to figure out the meaning of life. . . . I sat down with him and shared my philosophy," Jenkins recalled in a later interview. "That means a lot to me. When these kids grow up and remember something I had shared with them 30 years before that helped them, I know I'm living a blessed life."

Some of his ability to foster change was his use of timing. The phrase "When the student is ready the master will appear" applied to Jenkins' inspirational seminars. On more than one occasion, Jenkins visited local prisons to speak with the inmates. After one prison talk, Jenkins said, "one prisoner said to me, 'I never associated behavior with my attitude.' I responded, 'Behavior is the visible expression of attitude.' If your attitude is not being corrected . . . you will just go back to the behaviors that got you here to begin with." And from time to time, even in the prison setting, Jenkins' message hit home so powerfully that real change ensued. He had street cred. He was a World Champion in karate. His life was a road map for prisoners who had also grown up poor and disadvantaged. Listening to John Jenkins could be a turning point in a troubled life.

But there may have been another factor in his success; Jenkins did not consider his motivational speaking to be a one-and-done endeavor. He encouraged those attending his seminars to call him. Enthusiasm was a good start, but without commitment and hard work, it often faded into yet another feel-good moment. His decades as a sensei at his karate studio imbued him with the belief that real change comes with discipline, and discipline was a skill that could be taught. Follow-up was important, and Jenkins was happy to provide that guidance.

And people called. He never hired a secretary for PepTalk, and often as not, it would be John Jenkins himself answering the phone to chat. When Motorola released an inexpensive flip phone in 1996, Jenkins became even more accessible. He was a one-man business, scheduling personal consultations or booking business seminars for several hundred. Ann Parker smiled when she recalled his cell phone voice mail: "You have reached PepTalk. We are not available but if you leave a brief message, we will return your call shortly." "We?" Ann would laugh. "We?"

As his reputation spread, he took on speaking opportunities out-of-state and was invited to Japan and China. CBS News offered him a part-time job as a wellness/safety consultant. The New England Association of Schools and Colleges invited him to be on the board of trustees.

By 2001, Jenkins was 49 years old and had transitioned from competing at the highest levels in karate to the gentler practice of Tai Chi. In between he had won a World Karate/Jiu-Jitsu championship in Trinidad in 1985 and picked up the art of fencing. His knees and hips had been injured and reinjured during years of training and competition. He would later require bilateral knee replacements. He no longer gave public demonstrations in his gi, instead preferring a suit and tie. He continued very much in the public eye. His transition from world-class athlete to public speaker and politician was complete.

6

Somali Immigration to Lewiston and a Return to Politics

I n February of 2001, with the relocation of a Somali family from Portland to Lewiston, Lewiston began a remarkable transformation. Within 12 months, more than 1,000 Somali resided in the city. Ten years later (according to the U.S. census), out of a population of roughly 36,000, an estimated 3,000 were Somali. Previous to this, Portland was nearly alone among Maine's cities and towns as a destination for asylum seekers and immigrants. In a state in which 97 percent of the population was white, Portland had evolved into a mosaic of many races, religions, and ethnic groups.

As the cost of living, particularly for housing, steadily rose in Portland, Somali leaders began looking for other options for a place to settle. Word spread that Lewiston had a low crime rate, good schools and cheap housing. Perhaps the success of Portland could be duplicated in Lewiston?

The Somali influx was not without controversy. Some residents of Lewiston worried about the cost of providing services to the new residents. Unemployment in the city was already high. Anti-Muslim sentiment had been stoked by the suicide bombings of the World Trade Center the previous year. As the numbers of Somali in the city swelled, Lewiston Mayor Laurier T. Raymond wrote an open letter to the leaders of the Somali community, saying, "This large number of new arrivals cannot continue without negative results for all. The Somali community must exercise some discipline and reduce the stress on our limited finances and our generosity. . . . Only with your help will we be successful in the future—please pass the word: We have been overwhelmed and have responded valiantly. Now we need breathing room. Our city is maxed-out financially, physically and emotionally." (For an excellent in-depth review of the Somali migration to Lewiston, read *The Unlikeliness of It All*, by Phil Nadeau).

The letter became a lightning rod for both sides in the increasingly divided city. A neo-Nazi group, the Wyoming-based World Church of the Creator (WCOTC), planned a rally to protest the presence of the Somali. Its leader, Matt Hale, had been arrested a week prior to the rally and was later convicted of trying to have a judge killed. A pro-diversity group—Many and One—scheduled a counter rally supporting Somali immigration. Both rallies were scheduled for the same Saturday morning of January 11, 2003.

At the Many and One rally at Bates College, more than 4,000 attendees, including representatives from the Mi'kmaq tribe, students and community groups, labor unions, churches, and Black rights organizations, filled the Merrill Gymnasium. Maine's U.S. Sens. Olympia Snowe and Susan Collins and Maine Gov. John Baldacci spoke. Former Mayor John Jenkins was the master of ceremonies. Beneath his suit, he wore a bullet-proof vest provided by the Lewiston Police Department. His partner, Ann Parker, had a security detail assigned to her, along with the K-9 unit and an escape plan (as a white woman, she was a potential target). It was an inspiring event and, at the same time, a nerve-wracking one. Ann remembers going home with John afterward, holding each other, grateful to be part of such a special event, proud to be part of this community, and sharing tears of relief that it had gone smoothly and that they were both still alive and well.

Only 32 anti-Somali demonstrators gathered at a National Guard building across town, while more than 200 opponents of the World Church of the Creator demonstrated outside. When the white supremacist rally was finished, police whisked them out the back door of the building to avoid a confrontation. The overwhelming majority of the Lewiston community had made themselves clear: the Somali were welcome and intolerance was not.

Jenkins later compared the Somali influx to earlier arrivals in Lewiston—the largely Catholic French-Canadians. Both groups had left their homelands for the possibility of a better life. Both groups spoke a foreign language and practiced a poorly understood religion. Jenkins marveled, "That was a huge step away from all that which had been known into . . . the unknown. But they stepped forward anyway. Has there been friction between cultures? Yes, there has, but I have to

Our Finest Hour

Dear Family of Humanity,

This challenge to our very existence will give rise to our finest hour of compassion, civility, and community.

Where possible, we turn to our leaders for guidance.

JOHN JENKINS BACK IN BALANCE

Out of necessity, we turn to skilled professionals to provide clear, accurate, and life-saving information for guidance in making informed decisions.

Embracing the World of Change

This too shall pass. –unknown

Tornadoes and hurricanes pass. It is essential that we prepare for the after-work in re-weaving the threads of our new lives into a stronger social fabric to create community and a sense of belonging.

There is light at the end of the tunnel. –unknown

The light at the end of the tunnel is a mere reflection of our inner light showing through the tunnel of challenge, providing a beacon of hope for which to strive, and courage to keep making the next best step.

Just Have Faith. –unknown

The sun and rain fall equally on all. You do not have to believe in the sun in order to receive a sun burn. Whether you have or have not faith, we do have each other to help get through this and other challenges.

During this world crisis, we are encouraged to maintain our "social distance." Let us go the distance to be the entrance that invites friendship and community inclusion.

Our joined hands during to this challenge, are the same hands needed to help form a new community after the crisis.

In the hands of the people, resides the power. In crisis, it is how these hands are used that will determine if this is our finest hour.

Together, we must Strive to Survive to Thrive.

We Are Our Neighbors' Keepers!

In Peace, Well-being, and Friendship, *John Jenkins*

PEPTALK
PEPTALK

*John Jenkins provides tailored online seminars and services for all ages, abilities, & occasions.

Copyright © 2020 John Jenkins / www.peptalk.com

remind our citizens that (years ago) it was the Franco-Americans who were discriminated against."

One wonders if Jenkins, a Black man in an overwhelmingly white state, had, over decades of high visibility and public service, laid the groundwork for Lewiston's acceptance of the Somali. A generation of students had passed through the doors of the John Jenkins Golden Fist Karate Academy. Before each class they had recited the dojo-kun, an ethical guide for training in the martial arts and for behavior in everyday life. Their food drives and visits to nursing homes were highly visible and mentioned in the press. Jenkins' PepTalk motivational speeches had long been a staple in Lewiston and the surrounding communities. Had he opened the hearts and minds of some Lewiston citizens?

There have been setbacks: a pig's head was rolled into a Lewiston mosque (pork is an abomination in the Muslim culture). Tensions erupted episodically between African and white Lewiston youth, most notably, a fight at Kennedy Park near the Golden Fist dojo, that led to the death of Donald Giusti, who died after being struck by a rock.

But as Cynthia Anderson wrote in her *Christian Science Monitor* cover story in 2019, "Refugees poured into my state. Here's how it changed me. "It is easy to focus on the high-profile racist incidents and lose track of the largely successful integration between the old and the new. There has been a quiet, steady shift in the city, Somalis stocking shelves at the supermarket, white and Black kids sitting together at the library, white people buying goat meat on Lisbon Street. A high school acquaintance who had a daughter in kindergarten with Somali children was happy about the new diversity. 'I only knew white kids when I was growing up,' he said. After one member of a Somali kindergartener's family came home to find 'Get Out' scrawled on their apartment building, longtime residents helped paint over it. They worked late into the night, he said, so the message would be gone when kids left for school in the morning."

In Lewiston, a new wave of Black leaders has stepped to the forefront. Fatuma Hussein, from one of the first Somali families to relocate to Lewiston, established the United Somali Women of Maine Center in 2002. Later renamed "The Immigrant Resource Center of Maine," the mission has expanded to providing advocacy training, access to services, and education to overcome language barriers.

Following his tenure as mayor of Lewiston and time in the State Senate in the late 1990s, Jenkins was seemingly done with politics. Pep-Talk was thriving, and he now lived in Auburn, across the Androscoggin River from Lewiston. For a man who thrived in the public limelight, he valued his privacy, and his rural home near Lake Auburn suited him well. Auburn residents Ginger Levasseur and her husband Conrad developed a close friendship with Jenkins and his partner, Ann Parker, and often invited them over for dinner. The Franco-American couple first met Jenkins when their son was being bullied, and they signed him up for a karate class. They had marveled at the changes they had seen in their son as he absorbed and practiced the discipline of karate. Years later, John Jenkins officiated at their son Tom's wedding.

Conrad had a big garden that Jenkins, "being a healthy eater," loved to check out. Conrad even went so far as to offer to rototill a garden for Jenkins, but Jenkins declined. Ginger, now in her 80s, remembers Jenkins as having "an inner peace. We saw that and loved him." One fall, Jenkins went to the Levasseurs' home for Thanksgiving dinner. Conrad, who would sit and knit in the evenings, gave Jenkins a beautiful blanket. Ginger remembers, "John cried at the gift."

He and Ann often visited Harold Williams, a former security guard at Bates College, who had befriended Jenkins during a particularly difficult time in Jenkins' life. Williams' son had attended classes at Jenkins' karate studio, and Harold taught Jenkins how to play the guitar and sponsored him to join the Masons, a fraternal organization.

Jenkins lived a quiet life in Auburn until controversy erupted during Auburn Mayor Norm Guay's administration in 2006. Jenkins attended one of the public meetings and was eventually convinced to run for mayor. Similar to his campaigns in Lewiston, he won by a large margin.

The stipend for mayor of Auburn was just $1,500, but Jenkins dove into the job. Perhaps he'd forgotten how much he enjoyed the trappings of elected office. He was seemingly everywhere: making appearances at ribbon-cutting ceremonies, speaking at the American Legion, entertaining students at local school assemblies. He enjoyed preparing community meals at the local Grange while wearing a distinctive oversized chef's hat.

Jenkins' administration in Auburn lowered taxes and explored ways to save money by consolidating services (when possible) with Lewiston. He lobbied the city council to bring back the popular annual Spring Clean-Up, which picked up broken refrigerators and stoves and recycled them. He promoted a mobile pharmacy unit to deliver lower-priced medications to senior citizens. Phil Crowell, who was deputy police chief in 2006—he is currently Auburn's city manager—feels that one of Jenkins' most important assets was his ability to develop trust with long-time residents of Auburn. "It made a difference when John Jenkins referred to the Somali community as 'our new neighbors.'"

Jenkins worked closely with the police department, developing programs to deescalate potentially violent encounters between police officers and suspects, long before these programs became a staple of police training in Maine. Crowell recalled one particular incident in which a mentally ill young man shot his mother and was outside the house brandishing a firearm while cars drove by on Minot Avenue. While Police Chief Crowell managed the crisis on one end of the busy street and closed off traffic, Mayor Jenkins arrived and was a calming presence on the other end. Jenkins showed up so often at police standoffs, that he was provided a special reflective jacket, emblazoned with the simple word: Mayor.

When his term was up, Jenkins prepared to return to private life.

Years later, in an interview with *Lewiston-Auburn* magazine, Jenkins was asked by Joshua Shea, "You were pretty clear about not running for that second term, right?" Jenkins replied: "Yes, because I was committed to only serving the one-year term, I purposely didn't submit my name to seek a second term."

Ginger and Conrad Levasseur thought otherwise. As election day neared, they mobilized an army of senior citizens, "little warriors," to encourage a write-in vote for Jenkins for mayor. They made buttons and handed out engraved pencils and talked up their campaign at coffee shops and department stores. On the day of the vote, they stationed volunteers at each of the voting precincts in Auburn and pleaded with voters to re-elect John Jenkins. To have any chance of success, they

Just as he did when he served as Lewiston's mayor, John Jenkins fulfilled his two terms as Auburn's mayor with gusto. *(Russ Dillingham / Lewiston Sun Journal)*

emphasized, not only did Jenkins' name need to be filled in correctly, but his address as well.

"We gave each potential voter typed information so their votes wouldn't be thrown out," Ginger recalled. "Eric Sampson, who was running against John, called the cops on us! It was raining and the police came and said we couldn't be in sight of the polling station. Conrad knew otherwise. He had brought a measuring tape and informed the police that the rule actually stated that we couldn't be within 250 feet of a polling place door. He held one end of the tape and the police the other: We were exactly 251 feet from the door." Jenkins won by more votes than the other two candidates combined. He was the first person to win a mayoral write-in in U.S. history.

In the same interview, Shea asked, "You were able to be elected to three major political offices in Maine without taking strong or controversial stands on issues. Was that part of the strategy?"

Jenkins replied: "One person's strong or controversial stance may not be that of another person. We each choose the fight, and the way we fight for our interests. I've learned how to disagree without becoming disagreeable. Opposition on one issue doesn't necessarily mean opposition on all issues. Whenever possible, I'm always seeking common

(Russ Dillingham / Lewiston Sun Journal)

ground to bridge the gap between strong oppositional positions. The people would experience far more gains if our elected leadership were more amenable to vigorous respectful discussion as opposed to entrenched political party positions of 'our way or the highway.' My preference is to commit to the path of peace and cooperation. When a strong stand/fight is necessary I commit to winning the fight."

Shea asked, "Plenty of rumors have been circulating . . . that you want to be governor of Maine. Even Wikipedia says you're a potential candidate in the next election. Are there still public, personal, or professional challenges you want to take on but haven't had the opportunity yet? Do you still see yourself living such a public life over the next decade?"

Jenkins replied: "Many have expressed strong support for my Independent candidacy for governor as they've recognized that I have the experience, passion and plan for a positive future for our state. I also realize that, in addition to these three virtues, it will also take serious financing to turn this dream into reality. Our team has determined that the current limited financing options prevent my 'jumping in' at this time. I'll continue to find ways to fulfill my commitment to public service."

John Jenkins gazes across the Androscoggin River to Auburn's "twin city" Lewiston. As the elected mayor in both cities Jenkins was ever vigilant in finding ways the two cities could work together. *(Russ Dillingham / Lewiston Sun Journal)*

A memorable day in Washington, D.C., may have played a role in Jenkins' decision to run for governor of Maine. On January 20, 2009, Barack Obama was inaugurated as the 44th president of the United States. Thanks to VIP tickets provided by Sen. Susan Collins, John Jenkins and Ann Parker had a close-up view of the historic event. In an interview that day with *Portland Press Herald* columnist Bill Nemitz, Jenkins said that Obama connects to mainstream white America because he speaks with people in words they understand about solving problems that affect their lives, and solving problems that affect their children's lives. "Do that," Jenkins told Nemitz, "and the racial barrier simply evaporates. It's transformational. It really changes people's hearts. It's not that you change them. They change themselves."

As Jenkins spoke, packs of excited high school students posed for pictures among the nation's larger-than-life memorials, oblivious to the cold. Rather than saying "cheese" for the cameras, one youthful group hollered, "Obama!"

"The issue of race is not even on their radar screen," Jenkins said, "And it won't be an issue as long as we, the previous generations, don't make it an issue for the next generation. If we allow them to see the world through their own eyes, through their own experiences, then, in fact, it will not be an issue."

Nemitz wrote: "Still, as much as today is about the future, it's also about the past. The first time Jenkins ever visited Washington, D.C., he was in junior high school. He remembers running, not walking up the steps to the Lincoln Memorial. 'I remember getting up there, exhausted, and realizing how many steps it has taken for our nation to get to this point,'" Jenkins said. Nemitz wrote that Jenkins, himself, had occasionally smelled the danger that comes with being a high-profile Black man in a society dominated by whites. Security was an overriding issue when he served as master of ceremonies for the Bates College rally called to show support for Somali immigrants in the Lewiston-Auburn area.

"Were there threats?" Nemitz asked.

"There were some issues there," Jenkins replied, going no further. "Did I dwell on it? No. Did it stop me from going further? No."

Even in Washington, D.C., Jenkins knew that violence could strike when you least expect it. During the weekend of the inauguration, Ann and John entered a crowded convenience store and Ann pulled out a $100 bill (she wanted smaller bills for the train and taxi fare) and asked the clerk if he could make change. Several men lifted up their heads and eyed Ann with sudden interest. Jenkins immediately put his arm around Ann, and, after paying for the snacks and bottled water, quickly hustled her out of the store and up the street, before reminding her, "We're not in Maine anymore."

Jenkins concluded the interview with Nemitz by describing a true leader as "compelled by a higher calling of service rather than listening to the threats from people who are trying to discourage you. This is no time for fear . . . it's a time for hope that Americans [have] somehow found the right man—who happens to be Black—for these troubled times." "This is his time. This is his moment," Jenkins said. "This is the moment."

In August 2010, less than three months before the Maine gubernatorial election, Jenkins announced his write-in candidacy. Although it had been 15 years since he had served as mayor of Lewiston, and he had recently ended his term as mayor of Auburn, he remained extraordinarily popular in the Twin Cities. Thanks to decades of public speaking throughout the state he had high name visibility. But in the world of politics, his two-year term in the State Senate had done little to convince his peers that he was a viable candidate for governor. By the time he announced his write-in candidacy, endorsements had been made and many voters had already made up their minds.

The reasons for his delay in entering the contest are unclear. As an Independent, he competed with another Independent, Eliot R. Cutler, a Democrat, Libby Mitchell, and the eventual winner, Republican Paul LePage. Cutler's self-funded campaign poured millions of dollars of the candidate's own money into a failed effort to win the election. LePage garnered only 38 percent of the votes, but it was enough to eke out the win over Cutler.

Both LePage and Jenkins drew votes from the same constituency, the Franco-American community. LePage was born in Lewiston, the oldest son of 18 children. He grew up impoverished and spoke French as his first language. As governor, his style of confrontation led to a record 652 vetoes—more than the total by all Maine governors over

(Russ Dillingham / Lewiston Sun Journal)

the previous 100 years combined. His controversial comments on racial minorities, the death penalty, the environment, and the LGBTQ community, could not have been more at odds with Jenkins' collaborative approach.

Following the election, Jenkins returned to his motivational speaking business and focused on a new business as an independent insurance agent. If he had been disappointed in his showing in the recent election for governor, he never spoke of it. He and Ann Parker continued an annual tradition with the "Wreaths Across America" program to collect wreaths made in Machias and truck them to Arlington Cemetery in Virginia to lay in honor on the graves of American veterans. It was a time of quiet reflection, and for Jenkins, who had not served in the military, it was a way for him to show his gratitude to those who served.

His past martial arts contributions came alive to a new generation of karate and jiu-jitsu fans. In recognition of his four World Championships in karate and jiu-jitsu, in 2015 he was inducted into the World Martial Arts Hall of Fame and the International Black Belt Hall of Fame. On a local level, he was inducted into the Lewiston-Auburn Sports Hall of Fame and the Maine State Sports Hall of Fame.

(Russ Dillingham / Lewiston Sun Journal)

When he was notified of his selection to the International Black Belt Hall of Fame, he said, "It's not the trophies. I've got tons of trophies. They're all sitting in storage. But to effect a change of life for folks in a positive way, there's no better legacy than that. I'm so grateful to receive this honor. The profound thing is that so many people, unsung heroes, I wish they were here to receive this award," Jenkins said. "It was their hand that guided me to where I am now. I am so grateful for those who carried me to this point."

That same year, the State of Maine and the 127th Legislature created an official "sentiment/recognition" and requested his presence in the visitors' gallery. At the conclusion of the ceremony, Jenkins received two separate standing ovations from the House of Representatives and the Senate. Jenkins, who was touched by the recognition, said, "It took many helping hands and hopeful hearts that led to today . . . the praise is due to those who have carried me to this point."

By then, Jenkins had moved from the Lewiston-Auburn region, where he had resided since arriving on the Bates College campus in 1970, to Owls Head in mid-coast Maine. As his body wore down—he underwent bilateral knee replacement in his mid-60s—he transitioned from the rigors of karate to tai-chi. Ever the innovator and eternal

John Jenkins was inducted into the World Martial Arts Hall of Fame and the International Black Belt Hall of Fame. *(Russ Dillingham / Lewiston Sun Journal)*

optimist, he developed the Jenkins technique, combining the principles of meditative relaxation, yoga, tai-chi and brain/body research. "I'm trying to make it more of a nationally known program," Jenkins said. "It's helping people get centered. How do we operate at the highest level we can operate at? It's not about working out; it's about working in."

Traveling around the state, his PepTalk business expanded into women's self-defense with SAFE Plan in which he emphasized mental, physical, and emotional self-defense. He developed a course: Prime for Life, a state-approved substance-abuse prevention program for schools and businesses. He worked with police departments on methods of de-escalation, but even more critically, he instructed police on how they can avoid interactions leading to escalation in the first place.

But his lifelong fascination with politics was undimmed. Due to term limits, Gov. Paul LePage was ineligible to run in the 2018 election. Eliot Cutler, who had lost twice to LePage as an Independent, was not running in the race. Jenkins saw a wide-open field and was encouraged to run by long-time friends and political activists. While teaching part-time at Lincoln Academy, he sat down with the Head of School David Sturdevant and discussed his plans for another run for governor. "We had a good long conversation about it, and decided I would take a leave of absence," Jenkins said. "I could have stayed on and taught while also running, but that wouldn't be fair to either the kids or the people. Maine is a big state, and you can't run for governor part-time."

Jenkins, filing as an Independent, described his campaign in 2017 as a "people's campaign." According to the *Lincoln County News*, Jenkins felt inspired to run for governor due to a "sense of unrest" in government today. "If I were a sculptor, I would be creating works that speak to this feeling of anxiety. But I'm a public servant, and my skills are in building community and pulling people together, and perhaps that's what the state needs right now."

While traveling the state, Jenkins noted that Mainers in rural and urban areas had the same concerns: "Health care, homelessness, hunger, opioid addiction, and work. . . . Now it's about working together to find a solution and a statewide vision that can have local solutions." But once again, Jenkins' candidacy on the statewide level never caught the public's imagination. He was unable to reach the threshold of 3,500 certified signatures from Maine voters to appear on the ballot. In a state which had seen Independent candidate Eliot Cutler draw votes away from Democrats in two successive elections, voters weren't willing to risk voting for another Independent.

Following the election, Jenkins turned to his PepTalk business with renewed enthusiasm. He was invited as the keynote speaker for First Lady Barbara Bush's Literacy Conference in Waterville: Lifting Lives Through Learning. The title of his presentation—"LEARN Baby, Learn, So You Can EARN, Baby, Earn"—harkened back to his South Side High School days when Martin Luther King Jr. spoke at his assembly. King's speech, warning students not to give way to anger and hatred in the midst of police brutality and social repression, had made a lasting impression on John Jenkins. In turn, Jenkins passed on his message of hope to impoverished whites in Maine who were struggling to rise above drug dependency and illiteracy.

Jenkins was often asked to speak at churches. At the West Paris Unitarian Universalist Church, and later at the Norway Unitarian Universalist Church, he shared the theme of "Answering the Call." Drawing from Matthew 22:14, "For many are called, but few are chosen,"

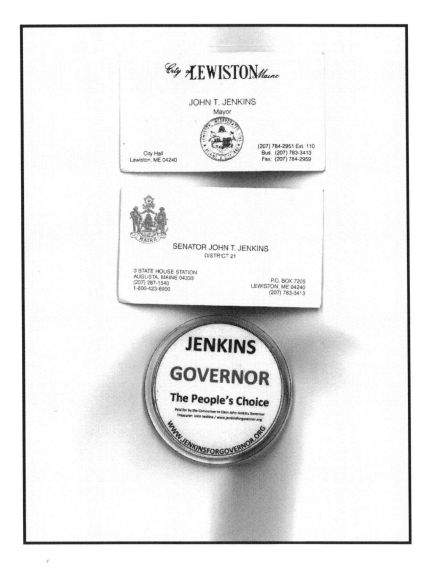

Jenkins connected the calling with a cause, facilitated by courage and faith over fear, in order to hear the call.

At the Patrick Dempsey Center for Cancer Hope and Healing in Auburn, Jenkins presented on "The ABC's of Contesting Cancer." He led cancer patients in the "Jenkins Technique—Balance In & Out of Life" program even as he may have been showing signs of his own health struggles. Jenkins was having abdominal pain and difficulty with swallowing. He sought out the opinion of his friend, family practice physician Pam Wansker, who was practicing in Greene. She recommended a series of tests, hoping that Jenkins had an easily treatable disorder such as a stomach ulcer. It was early in the Covid-19 epidemic, and Jenkins underwent a series of tests before the diagnosis was clear: esophageal cancer.

(Russ Dillingham / Lewiston Sun Journal)

For a man who loved to eat, the pain associated with the simple act of swallowing was debilitating. The cancer was aggressive, and despite treatment, it spread. He was admitted to Maine Medical Center in the midst of COVID-19 restrictions. Ann Parker was able to visit, but was not allowed to stay overnight. They watched football together as he received his IV fluids and chemotherapy. Ever the optimist, Jenkins believed he would beat his cancer. At one point, he believed he was gaining strength, and succeeded in walking down the hallway with Ann holding his hand. But the improvement was only a brief respite. For a man who had won world championships in the martial arts, he now needed her assistance to reach the bathroom.

The two had been a couple for years, but now, nearing the end, Jenkins wanted to marry. Scott Lynch, Jenkins long-time attorney and close friend, reminded John that a marriage license from the municipal clerk's office was required. Before that could be arranged, on September 30th, 2020, John Jenkins passed away. Ann Parker said, "We were married in our hearts."

(Russ Dillingham / Lewiston Sun Journal)

Over the coming days and weeks, tributes poured in. Newspapers, radio and TV newscasts around Maine provided special coverage commemorating his death. A small private ceremony was attended by immediate family and several friends, but in the midst of the Covid pandemic, a public funeral for Jenkins was not held.

For those who died during the Covid pandemic, final goodbyes from their loved ones were often unsatisfying and incomplete. Zoom funerals lacked the communal spirit of friendship and shared loss, not only for Jenkins, but for the thousands who died during this time. In Lewiston-Auburn, Jenkins' death was deeply felt. City councilors suggested that a way to honor their former mayor was to name a pedestrian foot bridge spanning the Androscoggin River the John T. Jenkins Memorial Footbridge. There was a precedent for this. In 2008, the city councils resolved to name a bridge connecting the Twin Cities after another healer, Bernard Lown, MD.

Both men worked for peace, Lown by founding the International Physicians for the Prevention of Nuclear War, and Jenkins by instilling in his karate students and PepTalk audiences, the lessons from the Dojo-Kun, an ethical guide for behavior in everyday life:

> *To strive for the perfection of character.*
> *To follow the paths of truth.*
> *To foster a spirit of effort.*
> *To honor the principles of etiquette.*
> *To guard against impetuous courage.*

While one man was able to organize physicians into a formidable organization, working toward a safer, nuclear-free world, Jenkins was at his best in small groups or one on one, molding hearts and minds. For many Mainers, John Jenkins was the first Black man they had ever met, and meeting him could be transformative. How else can one explain how a Black man from Newark, New Jersey, could become mayor of Lewiston? How else can one explain how the devotion of the Franco-American community could propel him by a write-in vote to become mayor of Auburn?

Unfortunately, after Jenkins' death, controversy erupted as to whether Jenkins should be honored. During the discussion to rename the pedestrian bridge in Jenkins' honor, one councilor, Leroy Walker, had his doubts. In the lead-up to the council vote, he reported that he had heard from people in his district "who were upset about what they were seeing" on videos from hurricane-hit areas of "Black people looting and breaking into places. It left a bad taste in everybody's mouth. [Some worried] that the city was only naming the bridge for Jenkins as a carrot for the fast-growing Black community." Backtracking, Walker added, "And I really feel bad because John Jenkins and I pretty well grew up together, and I know John Jenkins would never in his life ever be part of what's going on in these areas."

Amid the uproar, the story of Leroy Walker's outrageous remarks threatened to overshadow the unanimous vote (including Walker's), to rename the bridge after John Jenkins. In fact, for several days, the news cycle focused on the divisiveness Walker symbolized rather than the uplifting story of John Jenkins' life.

Thankfully, Ann Parker had the final word in a speech to the City Council a month later:

> *Two weeks ago, I, along with thousands of others, celebrated the announcement of the renaming of the footbridge in honor of John Jenkins. This was profound in so many ways: In his leadership of both cities, John acted as a bridge to bring the two together—not separated by a river, but joined by a bridge, now the John T. Jenkins Memorial Bridge. How appropriate . . . John was first Mayor of Lewiston, then Mayor of Auburn; he always had a connection to both cities and now, in a sense, he IS the connection that keeps the two cities together. John would be so humbled . . . and grateful—his legacy will live on, even though he is not physically here to brighten our world anymore.*
>
> *One of the things John would have loved most about this is that this was not political, it was both cities coming together in a collaborative effort to honor a man who was dearly loved and who contributed the best he had to offer to both cities. I was honored to witness both city councils vote unanimously in favor of the*

renaming of the footbridge. It was a moment of pride and finally something positive to think about in the wake of the enormous loss of John.

Unfortunately, in a short span of about 30 seconds, some words were spoken that became a distraction and then became the news. Instead of the headlines in the paper reading "Both Cities Vote Unanimously to Name Bridge after the Honorable John Jenkins" the headlines were a story about racist remarks spoken by Councilor Walker. How troubling and sad . . . I have met with Councilor Walker, the Mayor and City Manager and have expressed my feelings. The city promises to have training in diversity and equity and what is acceptable and what is not.

A sad irony in all of this is that the one person who is qualified to teach this and who the city surely would have called upon for such education is John Jenkins himself. This is what John did—he lived his life teaching others, whether it was young kids learning not to bully, or high school age to not do drugs, or adults learning civility, he taught others every day.

John was no ordinary man . . . he practiced what he preached; he walked the walk . . . he was a man of peace. John would not be happy, but he would not be vengeful. He would call this a teachable moment and begin working on his next program, troubled that racism exists in this day and in this area. He would want to move forward in a positive light.

We can't change the past; we can't undo what was done. We can only do better in the future. The very seal of this city of Auburn has the words "Vestigia Nulla Retrosorum"—No Steps Backward. I submit to you all to study that. Let's not go backward and forget the progress that has been made over centuries of trying to eliminate racism from our society.

When John was in high school, he had the privilege of introducing one of his heroes, Martin Luther King Jr., at an assembly at his school. I loved hearing that story, and John could recite the "I Have a Dream" speech—that one day he would live in a nation where people will not be judged by the color of their skin, but by the content of their character. . . . John had that character. He was a mentor, a teacher, a leader, an advisor, an influencer, a supporter. This is why he deserves the recognition and honor of having his name on that bridge.

Let's not forget that. Let us put our focus back on honoring the legacy of John Jenkins, and what he meant to both cities. Let us move forward with integrity and pride toward the dedication of the John T. Jenkins Memorial Bridge. I can tell you from my heart that John Jenkins lived his life to be the Soul of the City and the Conscience of the Community. I pray that others will learn from his example and follow suit.

7

Pictures of a Life Well Lived

(Russ Dillingham / Lewiston Sun Journal)

(Russ Dillingham / Lewiston Sun Journal)

(Russ Dillingham / Lewiston Sun Journal)

(Russ Dillingham / Lewiston Sun Journal)

(Russ Dillingham / Lewiston Sun Journal)

(Russ Dillingham / Lewiston Sun Journal)

(Russ Dillingham / Lewiston Sun Journal)

John Jenkins is seated on the left. Mel Donalson (with cap) and standing is Chuck James. James Reese (The Associate Dean of Students for International Student Programs at Bates College) is on the far left.

(Russ Dillingham / Lewiston Sun Journal

Harold Williams and Ann Parker share memories of John Jenkins' involvement with the "Wreaths Across America" program — which collects wreaths made in Machias, Maine, and trucks them to Arlington Cemetery in Virginia to lay in honor on the graves of American veterans. *(Chuck Radis)*

Notes

EARLY LIFE IN NEWARK, NEW JERSEY

Quote from Morehouse College President Benjamin Mays' eulogy for the Rev. Martin Luther King Jr. is from *Bates News*, Jay Burns, 1/19/2018.

Details about the 1968 riots in Newark, New Jersey, from https://www.blackpast.org/ Black Past Web Source and from "50 years ago Newark burned," NJ.com. Retrieved August 9, 2017.

Some of the reasons why Newark's African American residents felt powerless and disenfranchised are cited in *Report of the National Advisory Commission on Civil Disorders*, Bantam Books, New York, 1968, page 57.

Renaming of South Side High School as Malcolm X Shabazz High for the fiery former Nation of Islam leader several years later is from Lee, Felicia R. "Newark Students, Both Good and Bad, Make Do," *New York Times*, May 15, 1993. Accessed November 20, 2014.

References to Jenkins' father, John Jenkins Sr., being a deacon in the nearby Baptist Church and prone to violence are from *Maine History*; Volume 40, #2 "Lynching Jim Cullen," Article 3, "William Burney and John Jenkins: A Tale of Maine's Two African American Mayors."

John Jenkins' childhood memories of Newark, New Jersey, are from Pam Wansker, personal interview.

Details about Newark teachers' strike are from *LA* magazine April/May 2010, page 39.

Details about police treatment of student demonstrators at protest in support of teachers are from *Lewiston Sun Journal.* Posted July 11, 2015, USA International Black Belt Hall of Fame: Jenkins induction reflects on his roots, Kevin C. Mills.

David Boone's memories about Jenkins' interview with Dean of Admissions at Bates College are from personal communication, Ren Halverson.

ACADEMIC CHALLENGES:
THE BATES COLLEGE YEARS

First African American admitted to Bates College, Henry Wilkens Chandler, in 1873 is from "Tracing the Black Presence at Harvard," *Harvard Gazette.* Feb. 21, 1986.

Details about Gerald Talbot's lawsuit against landlord for racial discrimination are from "First Black Legislator in Maine to Fight Subtle Bias," *New York Times.* 25 December 1972. Archived from the original on 5 February 2021.

Lewiston Sun Journal's criticism of DeWitt Hotel's exclusion of Benjamin Elijah Mays from a celebratory dinner because he was African American is from Benjamin E. Mays | 150 Years | Bates College.

John Jenkins' reflection on a possible reason for his limited playing time on the Bates College football team is from "Walking with Giants" (linkedin.com), a column by John Jenkins. June 11, 2018.

The "town versus gown" dichotomy present at Bates College in the years just prior to Jenkins' matriculation is from Pam Wansker, personal conversation.

John Jenkins' close relationship with Franco-American employees at Bates College cafeteria is from Mel Donalson, personal conversation.

RESILIENCE

Mel Donalson, personal conversation.

A LEGACY IN KARATE

Details about John Jenkins' performance in the 1977 World Karate Championship are from *The Bates Student,* January 20, 1977.

Greenfield Massachusetts Recorder, Saturday, July 16, 1977; *LA* magazine April/May 2010.

PEPTALK AND POLITICAL SUCCESS

Jenkins' quote about why he stayed in Maine is from "The Griot: Preserving African American History in Maine," University of Southern Maine; Vol 7, Issue 3, 2004.

About labor in the textile mills being "just brutal" is from *Maine History,* Volume 40, Number 2, 6-1-2001.

Jenkins' quote about enticing Muhammad Ali to return to Lewiston for the 30th anniversary of his heavyweight boxing title bout with Sonny Liston comes from "The Night the Ali-Liston Fight Came to Lewiston," by Harvey Araton, *New York Times,* May 19, 2015.

Anecdote about Jenkins giving Ali a small city lapel pin instead of a "key to the city" during Ali's visit comes from Steve Cherlock, "Ali Showed He Was 'The Greatest' During 1995 Visit to Lewiston," from *Lewiston Sun Journal* (online), June 11, 2016.

Opening of Harwood Center on the Bates College campus: Online at https://www.bates.edu/harward/.

"Jenkins, John | The Black Past: Remembered and Reclaimed," www .blackpast.org. Retrieved 2017-11-19.

SOMALI IMMIGRATION TO LEWISTON
AND A RETURN TO POLITICS

Data about the number of Somali refugees living in Lewiston by 2011 is from "Perceived Barriers to Somali Immigrant Employment in Lewiston": A Supplement to Maine's Department of Labor Report.

For an excellent in-depth review of the Somali migration to Lewiston, read "The Unlikeliness of It All," by Phil Nadeau.

Quote is from Cynthia Anderson's 2019 *Christian Science Monitor* cover story, "Refugees poured into my state. Here's how it changed me." *Christian Science Monitor,* October 28, 2019.

Source of the information about Gov. Paul LePage's record 652 vetoes during his two terms in office is from Fishell, Darren, July 16, 2018, "LePage has vetoed more bills than all Maine governors since 1917 combined," *Bangor Daily News.*

Comments of Auburn City Councilor Leroy Walker are from *Sunjournal.com*/2021/09/08/racist-comments-tarnish-agreement -to-name-bridge-after-john-jenkins/.

About the Author

Throughout his years as both a primary health care physician and as a specialist, **Dr. Chuck Radis** has published both in peer-reviewed journals and in the popular press. He has written on the narcotic epidemic, the logic of expanding Medicare for all Americans, and medical marijuana. As the medical director for the Maine-African Partnership for Social Justice, he travels regularly to the Kiryandongo UN Settlement in Uganda where he partners with refugee groups in innovative public health programs. In recognition of his commitment to public health, Dr. Radis has been named both the Louis Hanson Maine Physician of the Year and Teacher of the Year at the University of New England, College of Osteopathic Medicine—a rare achievement. He lives on Peaks Island, Maine.